BLACKFEATHER MYSTERY SCHOOL

THE MAGPIE TRAINING

IRENE GLASSE

CAINE DREAMWALKER

To request permissions, contact the publisher at
projectcoordinator@dragonalchemypublishing.com.

Paperback: 978-1-7377292-6-6
eBook: 978-77292-7-3

Library of Congress Number: 2022933517

First paperback edition May 2022
First eBook edition May 2022

Cover Design by: Covered by Nicole

Printed by Ingram in the USA.

Dragon Alchemy Publishing
Frederick, MD 21701

Dragonalchemypublishing.com

This book is dedicated to the 2019 Magpie Class of Blackfeather Mystery School. Thank you for showing us we could fly.

CONTENTS

Acknowledgments

Irene Glasse

Caine Dreamwalker, for being the best crow-brother a witch could ever ask for. Blackfeather Mystery School is the product of a team and would not exist without both of us. I am so grateful to you, Caine. Ash, my beloved partner in all things, for endless support, love, gentleness, perspective, and patience while I struggled my way through a pandemic, a death in my family, and the creation of this book all at the same time. You are my everything. Enfys Book, without whom this book would not exist, for taking the 'Buddy System' to wholly amazing places. I am so proud of us! My wonderful family: Mom and Jerry, Gwen, and my father of blessed memory. It is an extraordinary thing to be raised in a family that prizes intellect, communication, creativity, and imagination. The chance of genetics made us related, but choice and actions made us a family. Kindred Crow, the musical project that keeps me sane, full of my crow-family, songs, laughter, and love. My many teachers over the years, through books and in person: thank you for lighting the path. I hope the candle of this book helps others find their path through the forest much as your own work helped me find my way. The Gods I serve, ancestors who watch over me, and spirits I work with. Lastly, and perhaps most importantly, to the students of witch-craft who studied under me at various points over the last 20 years: thank you for trusting me with your journey. A teacher is nothing without students to serve, and we always learn far more than we teach. Thank you. Blackfeather Mystery School is informed by what you taught me. You remain the best teachers I have ever known, and the best students a wandering pagan mystic could dream of.

CAINE DREAMWALKER

First and foremost, Irene Glasse is why my mad ramblings even exist within this book. The universe somehow saw fit to put this incredible human in my life who continually finds places for me to inject my special brand of chaos. For giving me the honor of walking at her side in this, my gratitude will forever be too deep to express with words. Bria, the keeper of my heart. Your love is the magic that manifested the warm, safe space I needed to find myself; to become Caine. The students of Blackfeather Mystery School for allowing me the privilege of serving as a guide and mentor. Taking up the mantle of teacher for these amazing people forced me to find ways to distill years of haphazard experience into something (mostly) coherent. Helping them to learn, and grow, has allowed me to do the same in turn. My goddess, The Dark Queen herself, whose arrival in my life a decade ago began the path that lead me here. And lastly, I honor myself for having the courage to walk that path as it gave me the wisdom and knowledge I now pass on to you.

BOTH OF US

Dragon Alchemy Publishing and Chanin Storm for taking a chance on us. The amazing test readers! Joe and Rebecca, Gwen, Cherif and Rebecca, and Strix. Jonathan Morrow for endless graphics assistance.

FOREWORD

If you have yet to meet Irene Glasse in person, make it a priority. I've been a member of the Baltimore, Maryland, Pagan community since the late 90's, and Irene has always been this incredible, grounded presence that pops up whenever the need arises, like a fae Mary Poppins. Whether it's a shop's Yule celebration, a local conference, or a chance meeting at Pagan Pride, Irene spottings are a bright spot in any outing. Her serene energy makes everything 'just right.' She brings these feelings of acceptance, strength and fortuity to a hectic world and a sometimes-confusing practice. In, 'Blackfeather Mystery School' Irene and Caine have blended a perfect first-degree system for those looking to experience an in-depth study of witchcraft, but who don't have access to a coven that meets in person.

Caine and Irene's wisdom reads across the page in a calm, authoritative voice that empowers readers to take the next step in their journey and embrace the practice that they're reading about. You see, as someone who has been a part of a community for decades, one of the hardest things I've seen for prospective witches is 'permission.' Whether fear of rejection from their families or peers, horror stories from those who have tried to find a coven and failed, and other pitfalls, it can be difficult to get 'over the hump' so to speak and make the leap from reading about the practice of witch-craft to getting to the practice portion. By laying out exactly what is expected from each chapter, and group of exercises, as well as what to have on hand, and exactly how long it should take, this book takes all the guesswork out of developing a consistent and well-rounded practice.

Many books talk about a few of the topics included in this book, but this is a fully realized and comprehensive guide to your first year of practice. The safety and security of all practitioners is laid out in easy to understand language as well as being one of the first lessons. It empowers new practitioners and reassures seasoned witches. Myself, I read for four years before feeling comfortable calling myself a Witch and for another three years before I decided to join a coven. Don't get me wrong, there is no linear experience model. Some are solitary practitioners their entire lives, some go in and out of group practice. It's all an individual experience, and that's one of the things drawing new Pagans: the ability to leave dogma behind if it doesn't suit you.

I'm always happy to work with a fellow Witch/Heathen/Pagan who is constantly learning in the way that Irene does. If you've attended a large gathering on the East Coast, it's possible you've already met her as a board member, a speaker, as a member of one of the bands playing, or while teaching a sunrise yoga class for the attendees. She is always engaged in professional development (one of the hall-marks of a true professional) and does this in spades. She is on the board for a regional Pagan conference and talks about her personal journey of spiritual development in her work with her local Unitarian Universalist church and its Pagan Pride day event. Irene is also well known as someone who writes a poignant blog that really targets wider experiences in a nuanced way. All of this makes for an instructor who has years of teaching a broad spectrum of personalities. I always feel seen and heard when Irene is present. No matter your circumstances, I know you will too.

In the layout of this workbook, the homework is my favorite part. Yes, I was one of those kids who raised their hand for every question, and I finished tests first so I could read my book. But this time, the homework really is one of the best parts. (Don't tell Chapter Five: The Witch's Cupboard that!) This homework not only reminds us what we've learned together, it does what homework is supposed to do: it builds on the themes of the lesson you just read, as well as the lessons before it. It doesn't feel like busy-work. The journaling includes really thoughtful prompts that help us learn more about ourselves as people, and as Witches. The oil making, the cupboard stocking and the activities are a lot of fun and help a lot with the learning process, but getting to put all that information together in a journal really helps cement the time I've spent with the book that day/week. If you have a friend to practice with, it's even more enjoyable with the partner exercises. I wish I'd had a book like this as a teenager with my first witchy best friend.

The timeless insights that Irene and Caine have included within these pages connected me with parts of myself that I thought I'd let go along the way. I'm happy to say that those parts were right where I left them, and I'm happy they've returned. I hope this journey allows you to rescue some of those themes for yourself as well.

~ Amy Blackthorn, owner of Blackthorn's Botanicals, and author of Blackthorn's Protection Magic, Blackthorn's Botanical Magic, Sacred Smoke, and Blackthorn's Botanical Brews. Amy lives in Delaware with her rescued pit bulls.

INTRODUCTION

When the Gods Give You a Homework Assignment

Within the wide world of divinatory practices, there is a form of Norse oracular ritual called Seidr. In that style of ritual, Seers invite the ancestors, gods, and spirits to speak through them. In April 2016, a Seidr ritual I attended was focused around the Norns – Norse deities associated with the flow of time and fate. Like the Greek Fates, there are three Norns – one that speaks for the past, one for the present, and one for the future.

If you haven't yet stood before a deity, or a human channeling one, it's a difficult feeling to describe. I liken it to standing directly beneath an enormous waterfall – the rush of power flowing before you is extraordinary, and can feel overwhelming. In that sacred presence, I can feel my blood pulsing in my face and a sense just below hearing, a sound like the roar of a river in my ears. I approached the seer channeling the Norn associated with the future – Skuld – and asked how best I could serve my community. "Keep teaching," they said. "Make them like you." I thanked them for their guidance and stepped back, relieved to be out of the 'blast radius' of that immense power.

My head spun. How could I make witches like me? My own path to that moment was meandering – years of studies based on my interests at any given time and the availability of different teachers, books, and courses. I hadn't planned to end up where I am. I just followed the Path and went where it led me.

I spent a year puzzling over that charge. I'd taught witchcraft and associated practices on and off for a little over fifteen years at that point and had never considered the possibility that I was making myself into any particular kind of witch, or that a course could be designed to do exactly that.

But what if there had been a plan? Could I get to where I am deliberately? What would that course look like? How would I structure it? The wheels began to turn. I brought on my crow-brother Caine to teach the spirit work portions. My own training in spirit work was recent, but I found the skills so useful and so complimentary to the skills of witchcraft that I wish I had learned them at the beginning of my path. Together, we hammered out an arc of study designed to be presented in four one-year courses. We began to teach. The first Blackfeather Mystery School Magpie training was held in 2019 to a group of around 60 practitioners. When almost the entire group attended all the way through the closing ritual, we realized we had created something truly worthwhile.

You hold in your hands my answer to Skuld: the physical result of a divine directive.

Blackfeather Mystery School is designed to open specific skill sets and traits. This book is for witches and aspiring witches who wish to work in community as well as with the gods. It is for people who desire a greater sense of connection with the world and Spirits around them. It is for healers – witches who are interested in healing the spiritual and energetic wounds in themselves and others. It is for practitioners who want to become more comfortable with and skilled at spell work and ritual. It is for those who are seeking a firm, stable, well-rounded structure from which to grow. It is for people who wish to bring their lives into better alignment with their spirits. Most of all, this course of training is for those who wish to become more empowered, stable, and sovereign in their practices and lives. For Caine and I, our highest priority is empowering you and the other practitioners sharing your journey. We wish to help you craft the armor you will need in a world that is desperate for healing – desperate for *you*. We believe that witches, spirit workers, and mystics like us will help shape the world to come. If we are strong, insightful, compassionate, and connected, we can build a more just and equitable world.

This book is for both beginners and those already on the winding path who are interested in filling in some of the 'gaps' that can occur in a practitioner's skill set. Gaps are normal and happen to everyone – I wish I had begun learning spirit work when I was 15. I wish someone had taught me how to set boundaries when I heard the voices of the Gods when I was a wide-eyed baby mystic. Every training system, every Tradition, every book has its strengths and weaknesses. With Blackfeather, I am introducing the skills I use the most in an order that would have been most helpful when I was younger and less experienced. I am trying to give you the structure and information that was not available to me, but that would have made my meandering path a lot more direct, as well as less dangerous.

Two Paths to the Temple

There are two ways to approach this text. The first is as a training course, complete with exercises to practice, journaling prompts, and homework. To take this path, set aside around two hours or so of time for each chapter. At the beginning of each chapter is a list of the materials you will need and any additional instructions or variables to consider. You will create ritual space (we will teach you how to do so in Chapter Two), read the chapter, do the exercises contained therein, and then close ritual space. Homework and supplementary exercises can be done in the week or weeks to follow. If you find you need more than one session to go through a chapter, no problem! Just pause wherever you are and close ritual space. To resume, cast your ritual space and pick up where you left off.

We recommend spending a minimum of a week practicing the material from each chapter. The first in person Magpie training met every two weeks and it seemed to be a good fit for integrating new skills and information. We discourage rushing through the training – take as much time as you need. There is no substitute for practice. In order to truly learn a skill set, the skill set must be *used*.

One of the many reasons that we teach grounding, centering, and shielding first is that those skills are vital to safely exploring mystical experiences. Many times, the parts of our soul and mind that are used in journeywork and spirit communication are a little rusty. If you find skills coming slowly, or find that you feel a little spacey and unfocused, allow more space between chapters and return to the daily practice. Go at the pace that's right for you.

The second way to use this book is as a supplementary source of information and skill development for practitioners who are interested in a particular area of content. On that path, it may be most useful to read the areas you are interested in and then choose which exercises and meditations to practice based on need. Remember to create a protected space in the manner of your personal practice for any exercises and journeywork you undertake. If something doesn't make sense or is difficult to access, consider reading and practicing some of the earlier material in the book. This training is designed to stack and jumping on the horse mid-gallop can be challenging.

How to Find...

Community: A good Pagan community is a true blessing. Being able to exchange ideas, practice, learn, and grow with those of like mind can greatly enhance both our skills and our sense of connection. Many times, the best way to locate your local community and find out about its gatherings is through your region's New Age and Metaphysical stores. Social media and the searchable nature of the internet is another good path to follow. Pagan Festivals, Pagan Pride Day events, and Witches Nights Out are frequently listed publicly online and are a good way to meet people from your region. Remember to use your common sense and watch for red flags when you're first exploring any community. Most people are wonderful, but the world of witchcraft is subject to the same challenges as any other spiritual path – sometimes abusers, manipulators, and other people with ill intentions (or unconsciously destructive behaviors) will find a way into a community. Ask questions, look for references, and observe the dynamics of the organizations and groups near you for a while before committing.

Partners: Some of the exercises in this book can be done with a partner or small group (versions for solitary practitioners are always included). Many of the community connections listed above can be good places to find people who would be interested in a study partner or group. Also, never underestimate your social circle.

Witches and aspiring magickal practitioners don't have one particular look or lifestyle. We are present in every segment of society,
but we aren't always obvious to the observer. If it is safe for you,
ask your social circle (whether in person or on social media) if any
of them want to join you. You might be surprised by who takes you
up on your offer, speaking as someone who has been surprised more
than once by who, among my social circle, identifies as a witch.

Help: If you find you have questions that are not answered in the
text, run into an unusual problem, or just want to talk to another
person in the Mystery School, Caine and I have both made
ourselves easy to find online. The internet shifts and changes, but it
is our goal to stay available on the larger social media platforms.
Our website is BlackfeatherMystery.com and we can be found there
as well. If you find that some of your work in Blackfeather brings
pieces of trauma in need of resolution to the surface, we recommend
starting by seeking out a good therapist. Magick is one tool of many
for healing. Therapy is a powerful tool for healing and integrating
our entire selves, and Caine and I both benefit from years of work
with our own therapists.

We are excited to be able to offer this Mystery School experience to
you. Caine and I have gone through both good and not-so-great
training courses. To create Blackfeather, we pooled the best of our
knowledge coupled with the lessons we learned from other teachers
and courses. It is our hope that the care and intention we built
Blackfeather with shines through for you. We are honored to be part
of your own winding path.

CHAPTER 1

THE FOUNDATIONS OF BLACKFEATHER MYSTERY SCHOOL

For this chapter, you will only need this book. This chapter
is lecture-based and should take somewhere between one
and two hours to go through. Your instructor is Irene.

Welcome and well met! The Blackfeather Mystery School is a foundational, full-spectrum training in Empowered Witchcraft developed through the collaboration of a mystic witch and a spirit worker. This training is focused on reducing self-sabotage while providing a solid grounding in magickal theory, dedicant or devotional practices, mysticism, spellcasting and ritual work, beginning spirit work, journeywork and much more. This Mystery School is a synthesis and outgrowth of over 20 years in the art and practice of witchcraft, and threads the needle between the structure of traditional witchcraft and the freedom of mysticism. Blackfeather is designed to create a safe, strong structure for the cultivation of mystical experiences for personal growth. We will be developing techniques that come from witchcraft, Wicca, spirit work, personal experience, and gnosis – contact with and knowledge of spiritual mysteries.

The vision for Blackfeather can be broken down into specific areas.

Empowered Witchcraft: Magick is a form of agency, a way of reclaiming our personal power from a world that frequently seeks to take it from us. This training seeks to develop authentic self-love and self-confidence, encourages physical strength and awareness, and teaches magickal competency. Through this triad, Blackfeather seeks to build a foundation of confidence and capability that will empower you to protect yourself, adapt to changing situations, and manifest your will.

Diverse Toolbox: Magpie Training seeks to lay the foundations for a flexible, useful skill set that can meet both practical and esoteric needs. By introducing the techniques of spirit work (sometimes referred to as 'second wave shamanism') in conjunction with the techniques of witchcraft, a more balanced approach to the world of spirit is possible. The two systems work beautifully together and enable access to a wide variety of tools to support your practice.

Underlying structure: A strong body requires a functional frame. Magpie Training adapts some of the best aspects of early Wicca and witchcraft to build that strong foundation. Repetition, ritual, technique, and study come together to enhance and inform your natural abilities. The result is a powerful, reliable underlying structure that will enable you to pursue any area of metaphysical study with more confidence.

This book is designed to be used as a course. Each chapter includes homework. To get the most out of Magpie Training, it is recommended that you work on no more than one chapter per week. Integrate and practice the work of one chapter before moving on to the next. Unfortunately, there is no substitute for practice. Think of the skills of witchcraft and spirit work as a muscle group – practice, repetition, and exercises to build strength are part of normal development. Those early skills also act as the base from which more challenging material can be learned.

FOUNDATIONS

It's so easy to put our own needs last. We live in a culture that demands almost constant attention, chronically overworks us, and encourages us to value ourselves based on accomplishments and resource-hoarding. When the measure of value we have been taught is completely based on external accomplishments, it's easy to ignore or delay work on our inner selves. Trying to balance our personal development against constant stimulation is already difficult. If you add in parenting or complex interpersonal relationships (or both!), it's a recipe for self-neglect. Our spiritual practices don't blow up our phones or show up on our doorsteps or demand that we help them with an overdue homework assignment in the middle of the night. They tend to fall behind in the face of the onslaught as a result.

That said, you have chosen to engage with a spiritual path that emphasizes inner work. It means that on some level you are deeply aware of the need for it. Paganism is not a path for people who like to be spoon fed. There's an immense onus on practitioners to grow under their own guidance. Pagan spirituality comes with homework – reading, learning divinatory systems, practicing spellcraft and ritual arts, shadow work, and more. Somehow, despite being forced to ride a noisy, uncomfortable, needy cultural merry-go-round of life, you have chosen a path of deep work and connection. This is good. You are instinctively reaching for more intense spiritual experiences. Understanding that impulse and the well it springs from can help fuel our spiritual practices in a more direct way.

That Which is Fed Increases

Our personal spiritual practices shape the kind of witches we become. This means that the contents of a practice support a particular outcome. Most witches, after the first few years, specialize in something. We become divinators, hedge witches, ritualists, astrologers, teachers, magicians and more. Moreover, practicing spiritual connection creates more spiritual connection. One phrase my mother likes to use is 'nothing creates proximity like proximity.' Now, that phrase was normally aimed at my teenage self when I tried to shut myself in my bedroom with a romantic interest, but the logic is sound. By cultivating closeness with the Powers That Be or our spiritual connection, we create stronger ties.

By regularly engaging with spiritual practice, we build the 'muscles' used for magick in its many forms. We become more proficient as practitioners. If we are dedicants (servants/allies of the Gods), our relationships with the Powers we serve become stronger. We are better able to choose paths that support our individual True North, our own natural alignment. As I am fond of telling my students, I am not good at rituals and magick because I have some unusual natural ability. I am good at them because I have had a lot of practice.

One minister I work with regularly has a saying I love: Practice doesn't make perfect, but it tends to make permanent. Creating and then practicing (and sometimes screwing up, changing and otherwise being human about) a particular spiritual form means that over time, that form becomes permanent. The trajectory of growth and development has long term support. We transform ourselves through our practices. We create the witches we become.

A daily spiritual practice is at the heart of Blackfeather. Your home practice will be laid out according to a specific design, but will evolve over the course of Magpie Training. Your home practice space will be used for daily work as well as for larger assignments and practices. If you already have an altar, you can establish your Blackfeather altar as a secondary space or temporarily shift your working altar toward the purposes of this training.

The Blackfeather Altar

Blackfeather Mystery School begins at the center – you. Your first altar in this training is a space specifically dedicated to your own personal spiritual growth. Through your daily practice, you will begin the process of coming into a better relationship with your own sacred self. To set up your Blackfeather Altar, you will need a few different items. Feel free to use materials you already have. If you need to purchase supplies, remember that thrift and secondhand stores are a great way to source inexpensive goods.

- A working surface. This can be a small table or transportable tray or box if you can't leave an altar up in your home.
- An altar cloth in black or white. These two colors support an energetically stable altar space. Choose the color that best fits your needs. For some people, a black-draped altar can increase feelings of depression. If you find that to be the case, please use a white cloth instead.
- A mirror or other reflective object that can be propped so you can see your reflection. The surface of your gazing object must be reflective enough that you can make eye contact with your reflection. Small, inexpensive craft mirrors and stands are frequently available at arts and crafts supply stores.
- A fabric covering for the mirror in either black or white. You will drape the mirror when it is not in use.

5

- An unscented jar candle. These are available inexpensively from most Dollar Stores and are often labeled as Seven Day candles.
- Matches or a lighter. If you live in a place where you are unable to light a candle, consider using a battery powered flickering tealight instead.
- An anointing oil or scent you would like to wear. If you have not worn a daily scent before, try a few different oils/perfumes/colognes. Many companies will offer small sample sizes of their scents for exactly that purpose. Each person's body reacts differently to different perfumes–it's part of why the same cologne can smell so different from one friend to another. Choose a scent that you like. If it's one that helps you feel optimistic, empowered, or comforted, even better! Feel free to experiment here. It can take a little while to choose a scent, and that's totally okay.
- A piece of paper with the daily Self-Blessing written on it.
- A small bowl of salt (regular table salt works fine).
- A dark colored stone that comfortably fits your hand. This stone can just as easily come from your yard or a nearby park as from a retailer.

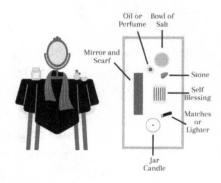

Figure 1: The Magpie Altar

THE DAILY PRACTICE

Magpie Training begins with establishing a simple daily practice. This first practice takes less than 10 minutes to perform and includes three parts: Self-Blessing, Grounding and Centering, and Shielding.

Consider the timing of your practice. Willpower is a finite resource – we burn through it all day long. It's much easier to make ourselves do something in the morning when our willpower is at full charge. By evening, it's sometimes all we can do to drag ourselves to the couch. If an evening practice is your only option, add a pleasurable component to your daily practice that will make it more appealing. One of my favorite tricks for this is to buy a box of decadent sweets. For each practice I complete, I get to have one of those tasty rewards. It's a nice way of reinforcing and rewarding constructive behavior rather than beating up on myself for a perceived failing.

Blackfeather Self-Blessing

Please print out or write this self-blessing to place on your altar. This working is designed to start taking the edges off the self-war most of us are fighting. When we are constantly attacking and tearing ourselves down, it makes our magick less effective. When pouring our wills into a spell or working, if part of us is actively trying to sabotage our efforts, the spell will ultimately be less effective. A deep and authentic sense of self-worth bolsters us as we move through this world. One way to start developing that confidence is through adjusting the messaging we send to ourselves. This technique uses the brain's neuroplasticity – the ability of neural networks in the brain to change – and helps reprogram our thought patterns with regular repetition. Even if you don't see yourself in this situation, this self-blessing is a good start on your practice – you might be surprised what changes it can bring about.

Light the candle on your altar, uncap or prepare the bottle of oil or scent you plan to use and uncover the mirror. If it's not already positioned so you can see your reflection, set it so that it is. Look into your own eyes in the reflection. As you look into your eyes in the mirror, allow a feeling of love and acceptance to rise in you. Look into your own eyes with love. If accessing self-love is difficult for you, cultivate an emotion related to it. When we hit the middle C on a piano and do not muffle the other strings, the higher and lower C notes also ring out. Similarly, when we access certain emotions and energies, other related emotions and energies 'ring out.' If self-love is not open to you, feel acceptance. If acceptance is not open to you, feel patience. If patience is not open to you, cultivate compassionate observation: witnessing without judgment or criticism.

Put some of your anointing oil onto your finger. Say aloud:

> I bless my body with strength. I am opening to my own power. (anoint your shoulders)
> I bless my mind with focus. I am opening to my own wisdom. (anoint your third eye – the center of the forehead above your eyebrows)
> I bless my spirit with vitality. I am opening to my own potency. (anoint your heart)
> I bless my blood with memory. I am opening to my own heritage. (anoint your wrists)
> I bless my path with mystery. I am opening to that which is greater than myself. (anoint your legs or feet)
> I bless my Self with sovereignty. I am opening to my own ascendency. (draw a crown around your head)
> By the Powers who watch over me, by the Powers living within me, may it be so.

The order of the Self Blessing is designed to support the priorities and goals of this training. You may eventually shift the order based on need, but it is recommended to begin your practice by following the Self Blessing as written.

Move on to the Blackfeather Grounding & Centering (preferred) or, if you do not have time, snuff the candle and cover the mirror.

Blackfeather Grounding & Centering

One of the most vital foundational practices in witchcraft is Grounding and Centering. This technique puts us in direct contact with the stabilizing energy of the earth. It realigns us to our place within the tapestry of life and reconnects us when we feel untethered. It is the beginning of every spell, ritual, healing ceremony, and working. Moreover, Grounding and Centering is a wonderful way to settle yourself if you are feeling unstable. Once you learn this technique, it can be performed quickly and easily whenever needed. Think of it as setting the stage for magick.

An audio recording of this Grounding and Centering is available at blackfeathermystery.com/recordings.

Close your eyes and allow your breath to deepen and lengthen. Consciously relax your body, starting at the top of your head and working your way down to your neck and shoulders....your chest and back....your lower back and hips...your legs all the way to your toes....your arms all the way to your fingertips.

Draw your awareness to your heart center. Notice a green glow radiating from your heart. This is your life force— – raw prana or chi: the magick that animates you and all living things. Become aware of the bright glow of life within you. You might see or sense that energy pulsing in time with your heartbeat.

Your heart center is part of a web of life extending in all directions. Become aware of the lines of energy connecting you to other life. They stretch in all directions – above, below, out to either side... These pathways hum with creation energy – the raw force of life. Allow some of the energy from the web to flow toward you. Let that green life-energy replenish your heart center, then expand to heal and recharge any areas of your body that need it.

When you feel full and connected, turn your palms to face up or out and gather the extra energy still flowing toward you by slowly sweeping your arms from your sides to up over your head, allowing the palms to touch. Draw your hands down to your heart, resting them on your chest. Feel your body incorporating that energy and returning to itself.

Whenever you are ready, take a deep breath and exhale on a sigh. Gently open your eyes.

Move on to the Blackfeather Shielding (preferred) or, if you do not have time, snuff the candle and cover the mirror.

Blackfeather Shielding

One of the challenges many witches and magickal folk face is an abundance of empathy and psychic ability. Almost all of us have the ability to feel what another person is feeling to some degree. However, as with any trait, the mileage varies. Psychic ability is similar to vision or hearing – it's a system of input with a variable range due to heredity and lifestyle. Within magick, a shield is a protective covering of your aura – the outermost layer of your spiritual and energetic self – that repels outside influence. It is protection for our psychic senses.

Life regularly brings us into contact with people and situations that can leave us feeling run down, agitated, or taking on the emotions of others. Wearing shields during those interactions helps mitigate the effects of that psychic or energetic bleed. To create a shield, we use a specific visualization designed to strengthen the boundary of the aura. Shielding, like Grounding and Centering, is an action that should be performed daily for optimum spiritual and energetic hygiene.

One note about the Shielding: this visualization uses green flames. If you find that green flames are not a good fit for you, you are welcome to visualize something different – briar, stone, crystal, a mirrored surface, or another material that can act as a shield. As long as you are easily able to imagine the shield, and it resonates with you as being repellent to discordant energy, feel free to employ it instead of the green fire.

A recording of this Shielding visualization is available at blackfeathermystery.com/recordings

Close your eyes and draw your awareness to where the lowest part of your body is resting on the earth. This might be the soles of your feet, your shins if you are kneeling, or your seat if you are sitting on the floor. About two feet below that point of connection, visualize green flames forming. These flames will form a barrier between you and the rest of the world, protecting you. Visualize those green flames thickening and beginning to spread up your aura – the egg-shaped sphere of space your physical body is centered in. See the flames spread up past your feet and ankles....your knees...your legs...sense them surrounding your aura in flickering green fire. Send those flames up past your waist....your chest...your shoul-

ders....sense them beginning to close above your head. Feel the moment when the flames connect above you, completely encasing your aura in green fire.

Leaving the shield in place, take a deep breath in. Let it out on a sigh. Whenever you are ready, open your eyes.

Snuff the candle, cover your mirror, and cap or seal your anointing oil.

Evaluating Your Daily Practice

Your daily practice should support your life. In its most basic, simplistic expression, you should feel slightly better after going through your daily practice. On hard days, that's enough. But the benefits of practice include the way it strengthens particular skills, capacities and connections.

A successful practice will result in a better frame of mind immediately after practice. That better frame of mind may last several hours or all day. Including a meditation section in your practice (specifically mindfulness meditation) can be particularly helpful for people who struggle with anxiety or depression. Over the course of this training, we will expand to include space for meditation in daily practice. However, feel free to add that part early if you already have an established practice. There is more information about meditation in the 'Meditation, Journeywork, and Strengthening Your Mind' section of Chapter Seven.

Over time, our practices increase our sense of connection to the Powers as well. This may include messages and visitations both in practice and outside of it (while dreaming or exercising, for example). Successful practices increase our skill sets over time as well. If you close with a grounding, centering and shielding every day, you will soon be able to ground, center and shield in a matter of seconds. As your practice expands to include journeywork, your ability to get into and out of trance and have productive journeys will increase.

Keeping a journal or otherwise tracking practice can be helpful in terms of observing changes over time. It's normal to wrestle with new techniques. Being able to look back and reflect on how once-difficult things are now more accessible is very useful. You will use a journal as part of Blackfeather – feel free to record thoughts and reflections on your daily practice.

Falling Off the Wagon

Sometimes, no matter how well we plan and prepare, life throws us a nasty curveball. Maybe we end up in the hospital or suddenly have a dramatic change to where we live. Maybe we wrestle with mental illness and go through a period where the invisible demons have the upper hand. Falling off the wagon of your daily practice doesn't indicate a character flaw, a lack of desire or incorrect practice. It just means you fell off. It happens. If that occurs:

- Meet yourself with love, gratitude and acceptance FIRST. A huge part of retraining our brains toward healthier thought patterns involves recognition and readjustment. If you become distracted 100 times during a meditation practice, congratulations! That's 100 times you noticed you were distracted and returned to your practice. The same principle applies to falling off the daily practice wagon. You noticed! You still want to do your daily practice! That's wonderful. Feel gratitude for your spiritual tenacity. Love your devotion to your spirituality.
- Set a return-to-practice date and prepare for it. If you realize you fell off and immediately want to start your

connection up again, then absolutely feel free to take a micro meditation (close your eyes and breathe deeply for two minutes) or light a candle. However, to restart your practice, plan for it again. Think of it like warming up before running. Once you choose the day to begin your daily practice, get ready by completely cleaning your altar prior to launch. This reinforces the pleasure of practice – clean, beautiful altars are inviting and enjoyable to practice at. Consider adding a new altar cloth, fresh candles or other items that make your altar even more inviting. Remember that Goodwill and other thrift shops are great places to pick up inexpensive altar dressings.

THE POWER OF SCENT

One good way to enhance magickal and ritual work is the use of built-in triggers for specific states of mind. When we regularly enter certain spaces, we begin to develop patterns of mind and behavior that are suited to those spaces. Subtle environmental cues cause the shift in mindset, and scent can be one of them. Scent is a powerful trigger on its own. Certain smells can make us feel safe and relaxed, remind us of our childhood, or induce less pleasant emotions due to their associations.

Blackfeather Mystery School encourages the use of a specific scent for times of dedicated study. When you sit down to engage with Magpie Training, anoint yourself with that specific scent. This oil or perfume is specific to times when you are actively studying or working through the rituals contained in this text. Your daily anointing scent should be a different scent than your Blackfeather scent.

If you live with someone who is sensitive to scent, consider opening and smelling the oil rather than wearing it, or putting a few drops on a sachet that sits near you while you work. If you find that you have a challenge with scent in general, consider using a different sensory trigger: a specific bell or chime to ring when you engage with Magpie Training could be a good substitute.

If you enjoy creating and mixing oils, consider creating one of the Blackfeather oil blends listed below. If not, choose an oil or perfume that helps you connect to a magickal mindset. Your local New Age or Metaphysical store will most likely carry a variety of scent blends to experiment with.

Blackfeather Oil Blends

There are six different oil blends developed for Blackfeather Mystery School. The recipes are similar but subtly different. In practice, we use almond oil as the carrier. A carrier is the unscented base oil that an essential oil blend is mixed with. Pure essential oils are very strong in scent and some can cause skin irritation if undiluted. Carrier oils have very faint scents or no scent at all and are often hypoallergenic (like almond oil). Some other options for a carrier oil are jojoba oil, apricot oil, or even olive oil. If you have a preferred carrier oil, feel free to use it. In an oil recipe, one 'part' equals a specific number of drops of essential oil. For example, in a 10 ml bottle, a part is four drops of essential oil.

The essential oils we selected to use in our recipes are designed to support the work of Blackfeather Mystery School as well as create a pleasing aroma.

Hyssop is a powerfully cleansing, protective herb, and is even mentioned in the Bible for its cleansing properties. **Patchouli** is associated with prosperity, spiritual growth, and protection. Moreover, its earthy scent is grounding for many people.

Chamomile supports healing and meditation.

Mugwort enhances psychic and magickal abilities. It also has protective properties.

Cedar is associated with resilience and longevity, and is often used in magick for protection and growth.

Lemongrass is strongly protective and aids in psychic development.

Clove is protective and supports healing and prosperity.

Fennel supports the mind. It is useful for studying and retaining the information one learns.

Blackfeather Oil #1	Blackfeather Oil #2	Blackfeather Oil #3
1 part Hyssop 1 part Patchouli 1 part German Chamomile 1 part Mugwort 1.5 parts Cedar	1 part Patchouli 1 part German Chamomile 1 part Mugwort 1.5 parts Cedar	1 part Hyssop 1 part Patchouli 1 part German Chamomile 1 part Mugwort
Blackfeather Oil #4	Blackfeather Oil #5	Blackfeather Oil #6
1 part Hyssop 1 part Patchouli 1 part German Chamomile 1 part Mugwort 1.5 parts Cedar .5 part Lemongrass	1 part Hyssop 1 part Patchouli 1 part German Chamomile 1 part Mugwort 1.5 parts Cedar .5 part Clove	1 part Hyssop 1 part Patchouli 1 part German Chamomile 1 part Mugwort 1 part Fennel 1.5 parts Cedar

If you are allergic or sensitive to the oils listed here, remember that you can also choose an oil or perfume that helps you connect to a magickal mindset.

To mix an oil, get a container with a dropper. These are available inexpensively at many craft, New Age, and wellness stores, as well as online. The proportion of essential oils to carrier oil is pretty small – a little bit of essential oil goes a long way. For example, in a 10 ml bottle, Blackfeather Oil #1 is only 22 drops of essential oil total. The rest is carrier oil.

Add your essential oils to the bottle first, then fill it the rest of the way up with the carrier oil. Seal or cap the bottle and gently turn it to incorporate the oils.

CHAPTER ONE HOMEWORK

1. Acquire supplies for your Magpie Altar and assemble it
2. Acquire or create two oils or perfumes: your daily wear scent and a specific scent for study time
3. Begin practicing the Blackfeather Self-Blessing, Grounding and Centering, and Shielding daily at your Magpie Altar

CHAPTER 2

THE BLACKFEATHER TEMPLE AND THE POWERS THAT BE

For this chapter, you will need this book, your Blackfeather oil, your Blackfeather altar, a device that can play a recording online (if so desired), your journal, and a partner if you are working with one. All exercises can also be performed solitary. This chapter includes both lecture and exercises and should take two to three hours to go through. Your instructor is Irene.

THE RITUAL OF STUDY

The more times we repeat a process, the more comfortable we become with it. Magick and Ritual are no different – repetition builds strength and capability. It also enhances connection; when you already know what comes next, or roughly what to expect, you are free to invest more fully rather than scramble to stay on track.

Each chapter of this book is designed to be a single class or unit of study, and each class is contained within a ritual. This ritual supports the learning process by creating sacred space and then offering the opportunity to temporarily set aside, or permanently release, any distractions that can keep you from being fully present with your chosen path of study. We come to witchcraft as complex, multifaceted beings with all the battles our lives entail. To get the most out of your time studying and practicing, use this ritual form to keep Blackfeather space free from drags on your energy and enthusiasm.

Rituals follow a set pattern. Part of what makes something a ritual, as opposed to a working or spell, is the repeated nature of the steps.

The pattern for the Blackfeather Ritual of Study is:

- Ground and Center
- Cast the Circle
- Release obstacles to study
- Guided meditation: Journey to the Temple
- Statement of Purpose
- Read the chapter and do the exercises in it
- Brief meditation: Returning from the Temple
- Close the Circle
- Closing words

Remember that if you need to stop your study session, simply bookmark where you left off, do the Returning from the Temple meditation, close the circle, and say the closing words. When you can resume, follow the steps from grounding and centering to the statement of purpose. It sounds like a lot to do, but once you know the pattern, creating and releasing sacred space around your study session is quick and easy.

Creating a Safe Space or Place of Power

The guided meditations in this book begin with visualizing a Safe Place or Place of Power. These vary for each practitioner. The place you choose to visualize should be one that makes you feel completely safe. It can be an actual physical location from a memory or a place you design and then imagine. The most important aspect of this place is that you alone are in control of everything that happens there. It's your launching pad, home base, and landing pad all at the same time.

My safe place is under a pine tree on the perimeter of a field I worked at as a day camp counselor when I was a teenager. This is a good example of a Safe Place. I am using my memory of a real physical location and then imposing new energetic and magickal rules on it. Beneath my tree, I am completely in control of everything that happens at that location. If something goes awry during a visualization, I can return to my tree and once more be in control.

A Place of Power is a designed and visualized location, or one that is found through journeying. Some people reading this book will already have one. If you do, feel free to use it. If you do not, Places of Power are covered in chapter eleven. Their use is vital to spirit work, so by the end of this book, you will have one or perhaps more than one.

OPENING AND CASTING

Please bookmark this page for use in each study session.

Begin at your altar and apply your Blackfeather oil (*not* your daily-wear anointing oil). Light your candle to signify entrance into sacred time. Take a few deep breaths and center yourself. You can perform the Grounding and Centering from Chapter One or, if you have a different centering practice, you can use that one.

Cast the Circle. Use your dominant hand or, if you are ambidextrous, simply choose which hand you would like to use for directing energy. The visualization to use for drawing a circle of protection around you is the same green flame used in daily practice. If you prefer to use something other than green flame, simply choose the same substance you are imagining for daily practice: briar, stone, crystal, a mirrored surface, or another material that can act as a shield.

When you cast the circle, stand up and point the index finger of your dominant/directing hand directly in front of you, over the altar you are facing. Cast your circle deosil/clockwise/sunwise, visualizing that green flame emerging from your finger and forming a barrier between your study space and the rest of the world. There is an accompanying circle casting chant. A recording of it is available at blackfeathermystery.com/recordings

> *Cast the flame the circle bright*
> *Sacred space contains the rite*
> *In the center power grows*
> *Within without above below*

Figure 2: Blackfeather Circle Casting Chant Transcribed by Scott Mohnkern

Sing the chant (or listen to it if you are first learning it) and cast the circle.

Releasing

If you have concerns that either need to be put on 'hold' for this session, or released completely, pick up the rock on your altar. Imagine your concern or distraction pouring down through your arm and into the stone.

A brief note about releasing: releasing problems does not magick-ally make them go away. It can temporarily reduce some of the concern around a problem, but if the root cause is not addressed, the stress and concern will return. Permanently releasing concerns is useful when you know your concern will not matter in two days, much less two years. Being cut off in traffic, having your child cop an attitude this morning, or your coworker wearing irritating perfume are all things that can be permanently released. Concerns that are rooted in trauma, deeper conflict, and challenge take more to unravel. However, you can set those concerns down – put them on hold – while you are studying.

Once you have channeled your concern or distraction into the stone in your hand, place it in the dish of salt on the altar.

Journey to the Temple

Blackfeather Mystery School uses an egregore, or energetic construct, to help all the Magpies, Rooks, Crows and Ravens in the School stay connected. We will perform a brief journey to the Blackfeather Temple as part of the Ritual of Study. An audio recording of this journey can be found at blackfeathermystery.com/recordings. You are also welcome to record the journey and play it for yourself.

Allow your eyes to come to a half-gaze or close completely. Relax your body and settle comfortably into your chair or seat.

Visualize your favorite safe place or Place of Power forming around you. This place is sacred to you, magick in ways only you can understand. In this safe place, you are completely in control of everything that happens. You alone have the ability to determine who can be in this space and who cannot. This is a place you can come back to anytime during this meditation.

You see an open, welcoming forest path forming before you. You hear the sound of wings and a rook flies past you, darting down the path. You follow the rook into the woods. You notice that the forest is dusky, similar to dawn or sunset. This is a time between, a liminal time. There's a faint green mist threading its way around the trees off to either side of you, floating just a few inches above the ground. You can smell the deep, rich scent of good earth and strong trees.

You see the path opening into a clearing in front of you. In the twilight, you see a huge circle of soaring stone arches rising from the soft green grass. At the apex of each arch hangs a lantern flick-

ering with green flame. Crows, ravens, rooks and magpies all roost in the trees nearby. This is the Blackfeather Temple.

The temple is a hub resting between the worlds. As you walk toward the temple, you realize that it sits on the edge of a cliffside, over-looking the mystery-filled woods of the underworld. The sun sets, half concealed by the horizon. This time is between all times, this place between all places.

Above the temple, beautiful metallic clouds in varying shades of copper, gold, and bronze are floating. These are the border between us and the upper realm, and there is an opening in those clouds directly above the temple itself. That opening is an invitation for travel, and an agreement amongst the ancestors and deities to watch over our work.

You walk through the archway directly in front of you. Inside the circle of arches are comfortable chairs in concentric rings. The Blackfeather Altar – a round, black-draped table – is at the center of the circle. It is here, in this space between all spaces, that guides and guardians come to aid us. Where the celestial healing light rains down from above, and the primal fire of creation fuels our spirits from below. This is where we practice. This is where we grow. This is where we stand united.

Take a seat in the temple. You may sense other members of the Mystery School sitting down around you.

Begin to deepen and lengthen your breath. Wiggle your fingers and toes, roll your shoulders, gently shift around. Take a deep breath in. Let it out on a sigh. Whenever you are ready, gently open your eyes. A piece of your consciousness will remain in the Temple and connected to the rest of the Mystery School until we release that point of connection at the end of each study session.

STATEMENT OF PURPOSE

Language is deeply powerful. When we speak words aloud, we are sending the intentions behind those words not only out into the universe, but to our listening self. It's good to explain to yourself and anyone else listening why you are doing something. This is why most public rituals contain a Statement of Purpose. Read aloud or silently the Blackfeather Statement of Purpose.

We gather to learn, to heal, to grow.
We gather to honor, to worship, to rise.
We gather to defend, to protect, to empower.
We gather to answer the Call.
Black feathers, green hearts.
So may it be.

That is the opening of the ritual. The closing will be covered at the end of this session. The center of each ritual is the course of study you have chosen – the chapter you are working on. This includes reading the chapter and performing the exercises in it. If you need to stop or work on a chapter in sections, simply perform the opening and closing of the ritual around whichever section you are working on.

THE POWERS THAT BE

The First Power That Is – You

"Before working with other spirits, be they embodied, disembodied (ancestral), or never embodied, the dialogue must begin with our most intimate spirit companion – our own spirit." – Orion Foxwood, *The Candle and The Crossroads*, p. 21

Blackfeather emphasizes the connection with the Self. The very first altar we create is to ourselves – it does not contain Godforms or ancestral shrines. It's a shrine to you. There are many good reasons for that, but one of the main ones is that we need to reconnect with our own spirits – our souls, or higher selves.

Your Spirit has a clear vision and deep knowledge for your life, uncontaminated by outside influence and upbringing. Getting into better communication with that knowing Inner Voice is absolutely vital. When we are aligned with and listening to that inner power, our choices are sound and our lives flow more smoothly. We are not struggling to cram our magickal selves into society's square, mundane boxes.

Right now, your daily practice is Blessing, Grounding, Centering and Shielding. It will expand, a little bit at a time, to create more contact space for your Spirit. However, by Centering regularly, we're already strengthening that connection. Take a moment to center yourself now.

Alignment Exercise

The process of answering questions more than once allows us to go deeper into the answers each time. When we write or talk out our own perspective, more layers frequently appear. We will use this technique for a contemplation exercise, centering on how we align with our own spirits.

This exercise can be done in two ways: as a solitary practitioner or with a partner or small group. Please have a journal available in which to record your experiences.

If you are working with a partner or small group, you will alternate the roles of questioner and speaker. Please choose roles and then proceed.

The questioner will ask: "(Name), When do you feel most connected to your spirit?" The speaker will answer. When the speaker finishes talking, the questioner will say 'Thank you.'

The questioner will then ask "(Name), when do you feel most disconnected from your Spirit?" The speaker will answer again. When the speaker finishes talking, the questioner will say 'Thank you.'

The cycle will then repeat, with the questioner asking the same two questions, in the same order. By repeating the question, we go deeper each time. And if the speaker runs out of things to say, 'I don't know' or 'I can't think of anything' is a totally appropriate response. The questioner will always respond to what the speaker says with 'Thank you.'

Perform this exercise in rounds of two minutes and then switch roles. Set a timer to help you stay focused.

If you are working by yourself, answer these questions in your journal or file:

> *When do I feel most connected to my spirit?*
> *When do I feel most disconnected from my spirit?*

Then, answer them a second time on a new page. If you feel like there's additional unpacking to do, you are welcome to answer them a third time. Remember to take your time in order to fully explore your answers.

Whether you worked with a partner or group or by yourself, take a moment to journal about what you noticed as a result of this exercise. What did you learn? What does it mean for you?

Powers Outside the Self

An encounter that does not conform to the known rules of consensus reality is frequently what causes someone to end up on the winding path of witchcraft. As a result, the different Powers – energetically or spiritually separate, sentient beings – are taught early in Blackfeather. Beginning witches do sometimes encounter them and it's good to have an understanding of the spirit world early on.

The web of energy of which we are all a part, and which you have been cultivating contact with through your daily practice, contains many different forms of "life." For the purposes of this area of study, what qualifies an energy as "living" is sentience rather than, say, a heartbeat.

Humans have three 'bodies': the physical body, the energetic body, and the spiritual body. Our physical body is our flesh and bones: the part of us that can touch and be touched. Our energetic body is our life force – the animating spark that is called chi, prana, or ki in other cultures. Just as physical bodies can be injured or ill, energetic bodies can sustain injuries or develop illnesses as well. The healthy flow of energy through the energetic body is an area of focus in witchcraft. Our spiritual body is our soul: the immortal spirit that we bring with us to this life and that will continue on after our physical and energetic bodies are no longer able to sustain us. Our three bodies overlay and interact with each other. One impacts one impacts the other two.

All three layers of reality intersect, not only within us, but around us as well. Our world has a physical layer, an energetic layer, and a spiritual layer. Sentient beings can occupy one or more of those layers, but not necessarily all three at once.

Also, one note before we begin exploring categories. Humans love putting things into understandable categories and organized structures. However, the nature of energy and spirit is such that those categories can only ever be rough guidelines, not hard and fast rules. For example, the differences between an Ancestor, one of the Good Folk, and a Landspirit get incredibly blurry at times. These rough categories are designed to give you a framework to help you recognize spirit or energy contact when it happens.

Corporeal Spirits

As embodied or corporeal spirits, it's easiest for us to think of the Powers in terms of their relationship with this physical plane. Corporeal spirits are currently incarnated in a physical form. They have shapes that are subject to the laws of physics as we understand them. However, those beings are not limited to the scientific definition of 'sentient.' Trees, boulders, crystals, and bodies of water all have physical form and many, if not most of them, also have an energetic or spiritual Self as well. Corporeal spirits can be interacted with on physical, energetic, and spiritual levels. As an example, you can hold an amethyst point (the sharply defined pinnacle of a crystal). You can wear jewelry made of amethyst. You can also harness the energetic properties of amethyst to help improve your psychic abilities. And, you can fall madly in love with one particular amethyst point because of the spiritual resonance of the Being in that stone. This phenomenon is part of why so many witches become deeply attached to their hoards of magickal tools. Many times, our tools are not just physical objects, but Beings in their own right as well. We would no sooner harm them, or throw them away, than we would our human friends.

Remember that all the other humans you encounter are also inspirited beings. Energetic and spiritual capability varies with predisposition and practice. Spiritual connection increases with practice. The ability to move energy increases with practice. These are 'muscles' that can be strengthened. However, all humans have a basic spiritual connection and energetic capability. It's why you can frequently identify who has walked into a room without needing to physically see that person.

All living (again, sentient) beings are inspirited as well. Communication with them is possible on an energetic or spiritual level, even if they do not have the capacity for human language.

Incorporeal Spirits

Incorporeal beings were once corporeal. They remember physical form. Since that is the case, they are the most understanding of the mundane challenges of being human and can intervene on our behalf. Some areas of human concern are simply outside the frame of reference of the Gods, i.e. finding a babysitter, dealing with a difficult boss, or negotiating the challenges of arthritis.

We have many names for incorporeal beings: Ghosts, Ancestors, Ascended Masters, the Hidden Company, and a handful of Gods who started off as humans.

Ghosts are generally characterized by their lack of context more than anything else. They are presences seen or felt, generally without an understanding of why they are appearing. Sometimes a ghost is an event that got imprinted on the energetic web that emanates from and permeates our planet. It replays when someone sensitive to the web encounters it. These are the apparitions that appear and do the same thing over and over and over again. There's no sentience there – just a memory. If you encounter one, you are essentially watching a recording.

Another kind of ghost falls more into the category of an ancestor, but it is generally unknown whose ancestor they are. This is the still-sentient, usually benevolent (or at least harmless) spirit of a dead human. Some very old buildings and other physical locations have them. This is where the difference between an ancestor and a Spirit of Place, or Land Spirit, can get murky.

The last kind of ghost (for the purposes of this discussion – this subject can get very deep) is a shell – a piece of the energetic layer of a dead human that did not transition out of life correctly. This is where meddlesome or destructive spirits come from. The energy body, or egregore, has the shape of the dead human, but not the soul of one. Normally, when a human dies, the physical body stops, the energetic body unspools into the web, and the soul transitions to the afterlife. Sometimes, particularly in cases of a sudden or traumatic death, the energy body remains, trying to finish whatever the human in question was trying to do. Shells can be challenging because they have a compulsion to remain. In cases where a ghost is described as malevolent, a shell is usually the cause of the trouble.

Ancestors have the greatest understanding of mortal concerns as well as the greatest personal stake in your life. They fall into a few different categories.

Ancestors of Blood are your direct family. Remember that even if the generation before yours, or before theirs, was a bunch of jerks, that is not true of your entire familial line. If you are a user of magick, or interested in becoming one, you are not the first of your line to be so inclined. Your Ancestors of Blood are why you are here, reading this book. Simply reach back further into your ancestral line to find allies within your blood family.

Ancestors of Milk and Honey are those who took you, or your blood ancestors in, as family. Most of us have an aunt, uncle or grandparent who is not a blood relative. In my line, my grandfather was adopted. His adoptive family are no less my ancestors than my blood relatives. The bond of family by choice is every bit as powerful as family by blood.

Ancestors of the Order are those with whom you share a life path or consuming purpose. These Ancestors are specifically drawn to those whose lives are dominated by the same energy as theirs was. Scott Cunningham is an example of an Ancestor of the Order of modern witchcraft. Freddie Mercury is an Ancestor of the Order for musicians. Michelangelo is an Ancestor of the Order for artists.

Ascended Masters can sometimes fall into the same category as Ancestors of the Order; however, their status is more based on spiritual accomplishment/adeptness than any other skill. Ascended Masters were once human, but their spiritual discipline has resulted in their transition to a status somewhere between human spirit and deity. They are possessors of great wisdom and knowledge, and can be petitioned/prayed to for assistance. Some forms of spiritual development cause a corporeal human to become linked with an Ascended Master.

The Hidden Company is a gathering of incorporeal witches, magicians and magick workers of all kinds. They can be attracted by good and powerful magick. This is why, at times, rituals can feel as though there are more 'people' in the room than the ones physically present. The Hidden Company can aid magickal and ritual work.

Once-human Deities have been elevated to Divine status through a process called apotheosis (Greek). Most pantheons contain a few humans elevated to godhood. There are a few causes of apotheosis: good works, marriage to a deity, and sometimes it happens simply out of chance or luck. These Deities are treated as Gods more than as Incorporeal beings, but they can be very good choices for petitioning for help with distinctly human, material problems.

Noncorporeal Spirits

Noncorporeal beings have never been incarnate in the way we, as humans, understand incarnation. As a result, they are frequently more skilled at working on the energetic and spiritual layers of existence than in the physical realm. Remember that these layers are connected, so a change on the energetic level does cause a ripple effect that has a physical result. An example would be successfully petitioning a God or Goddess to help you get a new job. That deity, a noncorporeal spirit, would address the energetic or spiritual roadblocks first. Loosening them would then cause a new job to open for you. However, that deity would not directly grab someone in the Human Resources Department by the hair and force them to read your resume.

Land and Nature Spirits fall into several different categories and those categories have very messy edges.

Spirits of Place are attached to a particular physical location. They can sometimes be a combination of incorporeal and noncorporeal spirits due to older burial customs. Burying a human in a sacred place already occupied by a Spirit can cause that dead human's soul to merge with the Spirit. Spirits of Place should be honored and gifted – they can help protect and draw good fortune to the residents of a particular area of land. Spirits of Place can also be Over Spirits of a larger area – the spirit of one particular forest, mountain chain, or set of lakes is an example. An Over Spirit (also sometimes called a Gnar) is the collective governing energy being for a particular species or gathered group. Just as all cells in a human body are part of that specific human, all individual daffodils are part of the daffodil Gnar.

The Good Folk, the denizens of Faerie, are such a large and distinct class of spirit that an entire session could be dedicated just to them.

Indeed, there are entire traditions of Magick devoted just to the Fae. The Good Folk are a race that occupy linked energetic space with us, and can sometimes manifest in our reality. They are variable in their inclinations toward humans – some are indifferent, some benevolent, some malevolent. Some of the Good Folk are associated with the Underworld. Some Ancestors join their number, so not all the Faerie Court is noncorporeal. There are countless theories about their order, makeup, number and kind. Moreover, some version of Nature Spirits associated with plants and wild places appear in folklore the world over. Depending on the cultural source, the information can vary quite a bit. There is also a good deal of overlap between Spirits of Place and Faerie.

Elementals are the energetic or spiritual manifestations of the primary Elements of Earth, Air, Fire, Water and Spirit. Witches can encounter both the Over Spirit or egregore of an Element and servants to that Over Spirit. They tend to look pretty similar and the word 'Elemental' is used for both, sometimes leading to confusion. They are referred to as Guardians or Watchtowers in some traditions of Wicca. Ritual invocations are generally to the Over Spirit of the Element. Smaller-scale spells often request the help of one of the servants. In guided meditations to visit an Elemental realm, the Elementals you encounter are usually the servants. Elementals are similar in power to the Gods and equally deserving of respect.

The Gods are the Divine powers of the different cultures of the world. They occupy the energetic and spiritual layers of reality and are more advanced and capable in those realms than we are. Although they can wield power and influence, they are not without limit. The Gods are not omniscient or all powerful. It is also important to remember that the Gods have their own goals, plans and needs. They are variable in their inclinations toward humans. Some love to form relationships with us and happily become part of the spiritual co-creative process of a human dedicant. Some fall more into the category of user – they find human dedicants useful when they are trying to accomplish something on the physical plane. Gods are best approached with respect and caution.

IF YOU ENCOUNTER A SPIRIT

Spirit encounters are uniformly startling, especially if you are not expecting one or have never had one before. It's normal to be caught off guard. If you can realize what's happening in the moment, the most important thing to remember is *you do not have to agree to anything they ask*. You can respectfully request time to think it over. Gods, particularly, have a tendency to come stomping in and demand your allegiance. You are under no obligation to give it to them. The practitioners who have healthy relationships with the deities they serve have negotiated or developed a respectful structure for that relationship. If you find a meditation, ritual, labyrinth walk or random mundane activity suddenly invaded by a Spirit, there are a few things you can do.

You can respectfully ask questions of Spirits to help determine who and what they are. Some examples of good questions:

"Where do you come from?"
"Is the form I perceive your true form?"
"What names do you go by?"
"What is your desire in contacting me?"
"How are we connected?"

You can run the entire encounter through your logic circuits. Sometimes people will externalize a part of themselves they can't deal with and perceive contact from it as Spirit contact. If a Spirit is asking you to harm yourself or others, or is demanding that you act in ways that strike you as selfish or destructive (getting plastic surgery, attempting to have an intimate relationship outside of the consent of all affected parties), you may be experiencing a piece of suppressed personality. Some spirits have also been known to try to masquerade as Gods for less than honorable purposes. If you have been contacted by a spirit that claims to be a deity, learn about the deity in question. Once you are informed about the deity, you can often tell whether or not the spirit is being truthful.

You can tell Spirits 'No.' Especially if they are trying to compel your service. Being in service to a God or spirit is a mixed bag and should only be entered into with full consent.

You can negotiate an agreement after research and consideration. If a Spirit contacts you and you do wish to pursue a relationship with them, learn all about them first. If it's an ancestor, try to track down as much information about them as you can. If it's one of the Good Folk, or a God, learn their myths and look online for other contemporary encounters with them. Then, determine what your own needs in a relationship with them would be.

You can hit the 'pause' button. You can flat-out tell a Spirit that you are not ready to talk with them at this point, but that you would like to have a conversation in the future, and give them a time (a year and a day is frequently a good choice).

After a Spirit encounter, as soon as you are able to do so, record what you recall of the entire experience in video, audio, or writing. Encounters that occur primarily on the spiritual and energetic planes tend to dissipate quickly in human consciousness.

CLOSING THE RITUAL OF STUDY

To close each study session, return briefly to the Blackfeather Temple. Sit comfortably in your chair and close your eyes.

Become aware that you are sitting in two places – where your physical body is right now, and also in your chair in the Temple. See the soaring arches around you, the concentric circles of chairs. See the metallic clouds floating above us. Hear the rustle of the wings of the magpies, rooks, crows and ravens in the trees nearby. See the black-draped altar in the center.

Rise from your seat in the Temple and return to your Safe Place, your Place of Power. Begin to deepen and lengthen your breath. Wiggle your fingers and toes, roll your shoulders, gently shift around. Reconnect to your body, to this space, to this time. Take a deep breath in. Let it out on a sigh. Whenever you are ready, gently open your eyes.

If you placed a concern on hold for the duration of class, you can pick up the rock from the dish of salt and reintegrate that concern by visualizing the energy you channeled into the stone returning to you. If you released something permanently, allow the stone to remain in the dish of salt. The salt will neutralize whatever that energetic burden was. Remember to change the salt out periodically, particularly if you find yourself releasing a lot of stress or discordant energy.

To close the circle, start a low hum and gather up the energy you used to cast the circle. You can either integrate it by drawing your hands over your heart or earth it by placing your hands on the ground and releasing it.

Read, aloud or silently, the Closing Words.

We go forth to learn, to heal, to grow.
We go forth to honor, to worship, to rise.
We go forth to defend, to protect, to empower.
We go forth to answer the Call.
Black feathers, green hearts.
So may it be.

You may want to bookmark this page for future reference as you become familiar with the opening and closing of the Ritual of Study.

CHAPTER TWO HOMEWORK

1. Practice the Blackfeather Self-Blessing, Grounding and Centering, and Shielding daily.
2. Begin memorizing the class ritual opening and closing chant and words.
3. Journaling Exercise: Look back at your journal entry from the Alignment exercise. What activities can you do more of to increase your connection to your own spirit?
4. Journaling Exercise: Reflect on any spirit encounters you have experienced. If you have had spirit encounters, what kinds of spirits do you now think they were?

CHAPTER 3

ENERGY ~ THE BASICS

For this chapter, you will need this book, your Blackfeather oil, your Blackfeather altar, a device that can play a recording online (if so desired), your journal, and a partner if you are working with one. All exercises can also be performed solitary. This chapter includes energy work exercises, so you will need space you can move around in (enough to stretch out your arms and take a few steps) and a snack for after class. This chapter includes both lecture and exercises, and should take two to three hours to go through. Your instructor is Irene.

B egin this chapter by performing the opening of the Ritual of Study on page 20.

RAISING, SUSTAINING AND DIRECTING ENERGY

Encountering Energy in the Wild

In the last two chapters, we discussed the three layers of reality – physical, energetic and spiritual. This chapter is entirely focused on the energetic layer of reality. In metaphysics, we use the word 'energy' to refer to the invisible force that permeates and animates our reality. This life energy is sometimes referred to as chi, ki, or prana in other cultures and traditions. Life energy permeates our energy body – it flows through us and around us and can be viewed as a circulatory system similar to our cardiovascular one. The big difference, of course, is that instead of flowing through organs and veins, energy flows through channels and energy centers. That flow of life also includes our aura: the egg-shaped space immediately around our physical body. This space extends several feet out from our physical body in all directions and is part of our energetic anatomy.

The energetic realm is similar to the physical one – it includes a planet and atmosphere. The atmosphere around us is full of interconnecting pathways of energy as well as places where energy has gathered. Similarly to air, there are places where the energy is healthier (harmonious energy) and places where it is more polluted (discordant energy). The energetic realm also includes energy structures for each Being within that realm: living, corporeal beings all have an energetic component. Most corporeal structures do as well. We can encounter, and sometimes cocreate with, the energy bodies of mountains, rivers, boulders, etc. Along with that, the energetic realm is where we frequently encounter incorporeal (never incarnated physically) and noncorporeal (once incarnated but no longer) beings.

Harmonious vs Discordant Energy

We have all been in spaces where the energy present in that space has a certain quality. One of my favorite examples is a room where people have recently argued. Without knowing what passed before, most of us, upon walking into that room, can feel a strange tension and unpleasantness in the 'air.' What we're really picking up on is the energy the arguing individuals cast off into the surrounding room.

The counterpoint to that is Holy or Sacred Sites. Spaces that have been revered, that have been a place for prayer, contemplation and some of the best energetic shedding humans can do, have a specific feeling as well. There is a beautiful, peaceful hum in the air that encourages contemplation and hushed voices. Some national parks share this feeling as well.

Another example is battlefields. Places where immense human suffering took place, even a hundred years ago or more, still sometimes carry the marks of that incident. Similarly to taking a backhoe to the physical earth, strong energetic trauma can leave scars on the energy field of a given location. Repairing the damage humans caused to that land, and its energy field, can take generations.

Energy of Influence

Another kind of energy we frequently encounter is Influence: the ability of others to assert or manifest their will on the people around them. For the most part, people who do this are unaware of it. Energetic interchange between people is normal. When I'm talking to a friend who is emotionally distressed, I am naturally giving them energy through listening and empathizing. Healthy relationships contain a give and take of that energy exchange – both parties support the energy between them by contributing to it in turn.

However, I can also generally compel people to listen to what I have to say. This is a more noticeable example of the energy of influence. Public speakers, ministers, actors, politicians, and anyone who regularly addresses groups of people has sharpened their ability to influence a room. The other group of people who have learned to do so tend to be magick users that lead rituals for groups. Learning to hold, sustain and direct the energy of a group of people is fantastic training for being able to direct influence with force.

Consciously directed energy

The third kind of energy we regularly encounter while out and about is consciously directed energy. Directing energy – using willpower to manifest change – is a normal behavior for humans. Witches hone the skill but all people can do it to a greater or lesser degree. When groups of people come together for a specific purpose, they apply their wills toward that goal. Macro examples of this are the Suffrage movement that secured the rights of women to vote and the Civil Rights Movement that began the dismantling of the white supremacy that we are still working to eradicate. Micro examples of this are new initiatives at a workplace where a group of people institute a policy or practice change; a family saving up for a vacation and choosing, together, to focus their will on that goal; and interventions: a group of people coming together to do a course-correction for a person they love.

Energetic Anatomy

When we direct energy, we primarily do so through our bodies. Our bodies are the interface between the energetic and corporeal worlds. For most people, that means we gather or channel energy within ourselves and then use either visualization or our hands (or a mix of both) to direct that energy. Our physical bodies move resources through our physical anatomy: passageways like veins and arteries and gathering points like large organs. Similarly, our energy body moves life energy through our energetic anatomy – an anatomical system that overlays the physical system. Different cultures have developed different ways of describing this energetic anatomy. The chakra system, originating from early Hinduism, is the most popular conception of energetic anatomy. Although many systems of explanation exist in the world, the chakra system is what we use here in Blackfeather.

The chakras are most frequently visualized as spinning wheels of light. There are seven main chakras in the energy body (think of them like the larger physical organs–the heart, lungs, and liver) and they are associated with specific physical regions, properties, emotional states and colors. Just as damage to an organ in our physical body will cause us distress, a damaged or overworked chakra can have a psychospiritual effect.

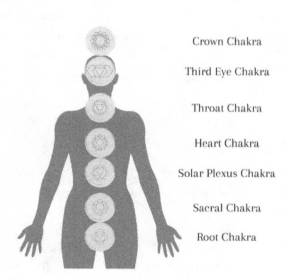

Crown Chakra

Third Eye Chakra

Throat Chakra

Heart Chakra

Solar Plexus Chakra

Sacral Chakra

Root Chakra

Figure 3: Overview of the Chakras

Chakra	Location	Properties
Crown	Top of the head	Spirituality and divine connection
Third Eye	Center of the forehead	Perception and psychic ability
Throat	Near the pharynx	Communication
Heart	Center of the chest	Love; not just romantic love, but love of all kinds
Solar Plexus	Where the rib cage separates	Willpower
Sacral	Just below the navel	Intimacy and sexuality
Root	Base of the tailbone	Survival and raw life-force

The chakras are connected by a network of energy pathways called *meridians*. The main energetic pathway runs along the spine and is frequently called the *central channel*. Additionally, there are smaller chakras, or energy organs, located throughout your body. They are called *pindalas*. The ones we use the most in magick are the pindalas located in the center of each palm and on each fingertip.

Just as a healthy flow of blood is important to our physical body, a healthy flow of energy is important to our energy body. Practice the exercise below, Energy Body Balancing, to balance your energy flow and become more familiar with your energetic anatomy.

Exercise: Energy Body Balancing

An audio recording of this exercise can be found at blackfeathermystery.com/recordings

Sit comfortably and relax your body. Allow your breathing to deepen and lengthen. Release any points of tension you notice as you breathe.

Draw your awareness to the base of your spine. Visualize a red glow there. This is the root chakra and it relates to your raw life force – your ability to survive. A strong root chakra helps us feel stable and grounded. Imagine that red glow growing brighter and

stronger. Allow it to expand like a horizontal disc or wheel with your spine at the center. Visualize that red wheel of light as bright, strong, and spinning evenly.

Draw your awareness to just below your navel. Visualize an orange glow there. This is the sacral chakra and it governs sexuality, pleasure, and creativity. A strong sacral chakra helps us connect intimately with others and brings new ideas into fruition. Visualize that orange glow growing brighter and stronger. Allow it to expand like a disc or wheel with your spine at the center. Visualize that orange wheel of light becoming the same size and brightness and possessing the same spin as your root chakra. See both wheels spinning together harmoniously.

Direct your awareness to your solar plexus – the space just below where your rib cage separates. Visualize a yellow glow there. This is the solar plexus chakra and it governs our willpower and confidence. A strong solar plexus chakra supports our ability to make and then follow through on our decisions confidently. It is also associated with manifesting our desires. Visualize that yellow glow growing brighter and stronger. Allow it to expand like a disc or wheel with your spine at the center. Visualize that yellow wheel of light becoming the same size and brightness and possessing the same spin as your root and sacral chakras. See all three wheels spinning together harmoniously.

Draw your awareness to your heart. Visualize a green glow there. This is the heart chakra and it governs our capacity for love and compassion. A strong heart chakra allows us to emotionally connect to others and both generates and attracts love and compassion. This chakra is also the bridge between the lower and upper chakras. The chakras further down the spine are associated with our basic needs and drives. Our upper chakras are associated with more cerebral and spiritual matters and the heart is the link between the two *worlds. Visualize the green glow of your heart chakra growing brighter and stronger. Allow it to expand like a disc or wheel with your spine at the center. Visualize that green wheel of light becoming the same size and brightness and possessing the same spin as your root, sacral, and solar plexus chakras. See all four wheels spinning together harmoniously.*

Draw your awareness to your throat. Visualize a blue glow there. This is the throat chakra and it relates to communication of all kinds. A strong throat chakra supports our ability to communicate authentically and compassionately. Visualize that blue glow growing brighter and stronger. Allow it to expand like a disc or wheel with your spine at the center. Visualize that blue wheel of light becoming the same size and brightness and possessing the same spin as the other chakras. See all five wheels spinning together harmoniously.

Direct your awareness to the center of your forehead. Visualize an indigo glow there. This is the third eye chakra and it governs intuition and imagination. A strong third eye chakra supports good discernment and use of intuition. It also helps us visualize, dream and see larger themes in our lives. Visualize that indigo glow growing brighter and stronger. Allow it to expand like a disc or wheel centered along with the other chakras. Visualize that indigo wheel of light becoming the same size and brightness and possessing the same spin as the other chakras. See all six wheels spinning together harmoniously.

Draw your awareness to the top of your head. Visualize a violet glow that shifts to white further from your body. This is your crown chakra. A strong crown chakra governs our spirituality and our sense of connection to the greater All–our Higher Self, the Gods, our sense of purpose and our true alignment. Visualize that violet to white glow growing brighter and stronger. Allow it to expand like a disc or wheel centered along with the other chakras. Visualize your crown chakra becoming the same size and brightness and possessing the same spin as the other chakras. See all seven wheels spinning together harmoniously.

Raise your shields to help protect your newly balanced energy body. Whenever you are ready, take a deep breath and exhale on a sigh. Gently open your eyes.

Directing Energy

Corporeal humans have regular access to three kinds of energy. The first kind is **personal energy**. This is your natural reserve of energy. It is created by your life force and reinforced by how you treat your energy body. Your reserve of personal energy is a finite resource. Remember that your physical, energetic and spiritual body are linked – what impacts one impacts the others. Physically taxing activities frequently correspond to a dip in energy. Not getting enough sleep, eating nutritionally poor foods, and neglecting your physical body has a detrimental effect on your energy. If you strengthen your physical body, you strengthen your energy and spiritual bodies as well.

Since personal energy is finite, we must be careful with it. We regenerate our personal energy (with a good night's sleep, usually), but it can really take a beating. When we get into designing spells later in this book, we'll talk about powering a spell. Because we use our personal energy to get through the day, it is not recommended as a power source for magick.

The second energy source we can use is **channeled energy**. This is energy we allow to pass through us for direction, but is sourced outside of us. Divine or Upper Realm energy is very light in nature. It is the energy we encounter in Reiki – raw, life-giving Chi or Ki –

and is frequently the energy we experience when in union with the Higher Self, Great Spirit, Gods/Goddesses and sometimes Ascended Masters. Channeling that energy requires forming a relationship with the source of it and then strengthening that channel. Most frequently, divine energy moves through our energetic body by entering at the crown chakra, traveling down the central channel through the third eye and throat chakras, entering the heart chakra and then moving out across the shoulders, down the arms and into the hands from there.

Earth energy is channeled energy that we draw from corporeal structures in this realm: mountains, oceans, rivers, crystals, trees, and plants are all examples. These energies also require the cultivation of a relationship with and connection to them. For example, it is less effective to try to simply dig in and grab the energy of a tree without first creating a bond with that being. Earth energy frequently follows a different energetic pathway in the body, entering from wherever your body is in contact with the earth (or the Being you are channeling), passing through your root, sacral, and solar plexus chakras, entering the heart chakra and making its way down your arms and into your hands.

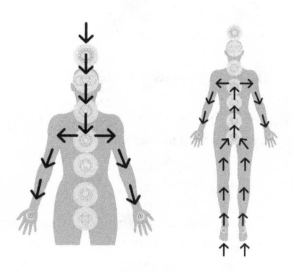

Figure 4: Paths of Divine Energy and Earth Energy

The third kind of energy we can tap into and direct is **Raised Energy**. This energy comes from the living energy field: the web of interconnection we tap into during Blackfeather Grounding and Centering. When we perform an energy-raising activity, energy from the energy field flows toward us and builds up in our bodies. We can then direct it. Examples of raised energy include chanting, singing, humming, dancing, and drumming. Raising Energy is covered later in this chapter.

Exercise: Return to Self Mudra

Energy work does have some risks since we are frequently in contact with energy that does not originate inside of us. The Return to Self Mudra helps us create a tool to help us return, fully, to our own Sacred Selves. A mudra is a gesture or shape made with our hands that has spiritual or energetic properties. This exercise develops your Return to Self Mudra. Going forward, you will use it at the close of any energy work. It's also useful for times when you feel out of sorts or out of alignment with yourself. There is a recording of the cues for this exercise at:

blackfeathermystery.com/recordings.

Please find a space where you can move around a little bit. You'll need space to move your arms as well.

1. Begin by repeating your name, your identity-specific name, to yourself softly.
2. Start to walk or move around as you do so. As you move, find a gesture that goes with your name. A movement of some sort. You can say your name more loudly now if it helps.
3. Simplify your gesture, so that it's just one or two movements at the most.
4. Now, make the gesture smaller. Whisper your name, and make the gesture a whisper as well.
5. Come to stillness.

This small gesture is your Return to Self Mudra – a key that brings you back into your body, with only your energy attached to you. It is used after energy work, rituals and any trance possessory work. It's a safety mechanism that draws you back to your Sacred Self.

ENERGY WORK CAUTIONS

There are a few things to remember when practicing energy work. *Ground and Center* beforehand – begin from a place of stability. *Set the intention* for the space and the work. Our intention this evening is to learn safely. The next one is a little silly, but it's quite true – *don't clench up*. Even when we're studying witchcraft, healing, energy work, and other modalities outside accepted Western thought, feeling energy move can be a little startling. Try to relax and just experience the work. As soon as you clench up, the energy you're channeling or supporting stops flowing. Then, when you're finished with energy work, use your Return to Self Mudra and *ground and center*. After that, *eat something*. It helps the corporeal body and energy body reintegrate with each other. Also, energy work is taxing. I'm usually starving after a session of energy work or ritual, so food afterward is simply practical.

ENERGY WORK EXERCISES

Experiencing the movement of energy firsthand is the best way to learn to use it more effectively. A collection of exercises for individual practitioners and small groups are listed below. Please perform all the exercises that are open to you. If you are working with a partner, read through the exercises first and then thoroughly explain what you are doing and obtain informed consent before practicing.

Individual Exercises

Our bodies are the intermediary, the conduit, between the energetic and corporeal worlds. So, we will begin by tuning the body for this work. Hold your hands in front of you, palm up. Begin to focus all of your awareness into the palms of your hands. You may feel a tingling or warmth. This shifting of attention is called sensitizing your hands. Turn your palms to face each other. Begin to experiment with moving them closer together and then further away from each other. You may feel a magnetism, or a sense of resistance.

Holding your palms facing each other at a comfortable distance, begin to channel energy into your hands. If channeling is a new idea for you, simply imagine life energy flowing from your body, down your arms, into your hands and through the palms of your hands into the space between them. Allow that energy to form a sphere. Experiment with this energy ball – move your hands across its surface. See if you can make it larger or smaller. What do you notice about it? What sensations and impressions are coming to you? Are you getting a sense of color or texture?

Draw the energy ball into your chest and let it integrate back into your body. Now, keeping your hands sensitized, begin to run them over the innermost layer of your aura – the layer that's about 6 inches to one foot beyond the physical boundaries of your body. See if you notice areas of heat or cool, tingling or sharpness.

Combining the last two exercises, go over your innermost auric layer again. This time, when you find a space that stands out, either due to temperature change or tingling, create a small energy ball with your dominant hand. Then, apply that energy ball to the spot you noticed. This is called patching, and it can be a useful way to shore up your aura.

Raising Energy

To power a magickal working, we need to raise energy. One of the most effective ways to do so is with our own bodies. As previously discussed, our bodies exist in the three layers of reality: spiritual, energetic, and physical. As a result, they are an optimum tool for generating and then directing energy. We have the ability within us to transmute physical energy – an elevated pulse, heat, or the sensation of fullness – into spiritual energy simply by consciously directing it. The flow of energy we experience at those moments comes from different places: our own natural reserves, the web of life that surrounds us, and the Earth itself.

The physical sensation of energy building can best be described as a form of excitement. When we raise energy, our pulse may quicken, our breathing change, and our experience of our body's physical cues will shift. We may feel heat or tingling, a sense of fullness, or a fierce joy.

Chanting is a wonderful way to raise energy both individually and as part of a group. For energy raising, choose chants that are fairly simple and repetitive. It's important to avoid distraction and worrying about what words come next when building energy up. A good example chant for raising energy is

Fire and Air, Fire and Air
Earth, Water, Earth, Water

To practice this form of energy raising, start by grounding and centering. Feel your connection to the web of life around you, the nexus of green fire we visualize during daily Blackfeather altar practice. If you are standing, allow your hands to fall comfortably by your sides. If you are seated, begin with them resting in your lap. Then, begin to speak the chant. Start at a soft or normal speaking volume. Slowly increase in volume and speed. As you do, allow your hands to rise to support the energy as it builds. Energy will flow to you from every direction in the web of life. When you have reached a feeling of 'peak' or fullness, stop chanting and draw your hands down to your heart center to integrate the energy you raised. Take a few deep breaths to balance yourself out, ground and center if needed. If you're still feeling too much energy circulating in your system, place your hands on the floor to release excess energy into the earth.

To direct the energy you've raised at peak, you have a few different options. Some people visualize the energy flowing out of their hands and into an object they are charging. You can also turn the palms of your hands to face the target of your energy and then release that energy out through your hands. This is useful for situations where you are unable to physically touch your target. One other technique is to use breath. At the peak of your energy raising, visualize the energy you've raised moving into your lungs. Take a deep breath in and blow that energy out into the object you are charging or enchanting.

Singing and chanting are very similar in terms of how energy is raised. The one caveat here is that singing can be uncomfortable for people who do not like to sing or who feel insecure about their voices. To raise energy through singing, select a simple melody. It does not even need to have words. Again, start softly and increase in volume, drawing energy in from the web of life around you as you sing.

Dance and movement are wonderful ways to raise energy. By increasing our heart rate and moving our bodies, we build a lot of natural energy. If you choose a repetitive or free-form movement, it's easy to concentrate on the goal you are raising energy for. If you prefer to work with music, put on a song you love to dance to or an uptempo drumming track. One simple movement pattern that is very effective is the cross-body reach. Start by standing comfortably if you are able to. This movement pattern can also be done seated. Aligning your movement with the beat of the song, reach one arm across your body and back, then the other. Bring your eyes to a half gaze or allow them to close completely so you can visualize your goal. Each time you pull your hand back to your side, visualize it drawing more energy into your core. When you have reached peak or fullness, direct the energy through your palms, with visualization, or with breath.

Breathing exercises are also an option for raising energy. However, it's important to remember that deep breathing and rapid breathing patterns can easily cause lightheadedness. Practice with your breath pattern before using it to direct energy in a magickal working. One of the simplest ways to raise energy through breathwork is to inhale deeply and as you exhale, visualize energy building in your belly. Repeat and allow the energy to grow in your core. It can sometimes be helpful to hold your hands on or over your belly as you're building up the energy. When you have reached peak or fullness, direct the energy. This form lends itself to using breath as your charging mechanic.

Partner Exercises

These exercises work best with another person. If you are able to practice with someone else, please do so, remembering to obtain informed consent before engaging with the exercise. Otherwise, simply read through these exercises for later reference.

Field Scan: Using the same scanning technique that we just used on ourselves, scan the innermost layer of the aura of your partner. Again, this layer is about 6 inches to one foot away from your part-ner. You will not need to make physical contact with your partner in order to scan their energy field. Pay attention to areas where there's a temperature change, increased or decreased tingling, or other difference in sensation. Then, tell your partner what you noticed. When you have finished, switch places.

Energy Ring: For this exercise, stand facing your partner. Hold your right hand out, palm down. Place your left hand a few inches below their right hand, palm facing up. This exercise works on creating an energy ring. Begin to gently send energy through your right palm into your partner's left palm. You may feel energy moving into you from your left palm. Allow the energy to flow along a pathway from your left hand, to your left arm, to your chest, to your right arm and then out your right palm. When you have finished, gently disengage and rub the palms of your hands together.

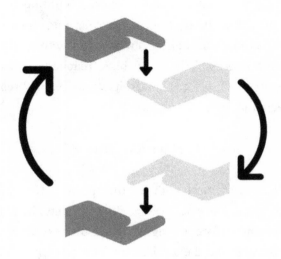

Figure 5: Energy Ring

Pushing/Pulling: Stand facing your partner, but this time stand far enough away that one of you can fully extend your arms without touching the other. One at a time, using only energy channeled into your hands, try to push your partner. Then, again using only energy, try to pull your partner toward you. Please be careful – if either of you feels like you are going to fall at any point in time, stop the exercise. When you have finished, share your observations with each other and switch places.

Group Exercises

Just as there are exercises that work better with a partner, these exercises work best with three or more people. If you have other practitioners to practice with, please do so. If not, simply read through the exercises to familiarize yourself with them.

Energy Ring: Standing in a circle facing each other, hold your right hand out, palm down, near the individual on your right. Hold your left hand out, palm up, a few inches beneath the palm of the individual to your left. Begin to gently send energy through your right palm into your partner's left palm. You may feel energy moving into you from your left palm. Allow the energy to flow along a pathway from your left hand, to your left arm, to your chest, to your right arm and then out your right palm. When you have finished, gently disengage and rub the palms of your hands together.

Figure 6: Group Energy Ring

Wheel and Spokes Healing: See if one of your group would like to receive healing. Whoever that individual is should stand in the center of your circle. The remaining members of your group should raise their hands comfortably, palms facing inward. Set a timer for two minutes. Remember the feeling of the Energy Ring, but keep your palms facing in, and begin to send energy around the circle. Now, using your right hand, or your dominant hand, visualize bright, warm, healing energy flowing toward the person in the center of the circle. You'll still be aware of the ring of energy flowing around the outside of the circle, but now the ring has 'spokes' – lines of healing flowing from the ring of energy toward the center. If the person in the middle feels overwhelmed or dizzy, they should say 'stop' and all participants will lower their hands, breaking the circuit.

When the timer goes off, all participants should lower their hands and ground and center. This is especially important for the person who received healing. If they are still feeling a little light-headed or woozy, they should eat a snack and drink some water to help reintegrate with their body.

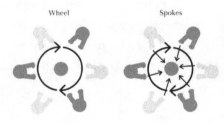

Figure 7: Wheel and Spokes Healing

Healing Circle: Once more, stand in a circle. Turn to your right so that you are all facing the same direction, and scoot in a little bit so that you can easily float your hands over the shoulder blades or back of the person in front of you. Remember the bright, warm healing energy from the Wheel and Spokes exercise, and begin to channel that energy through the palms of your hands and into the back of the person in front of you. You will probably be aware of the healing energy flowing into you from the person standing behind you. When you have finished, gently disengage and rub the palms of your hands together.

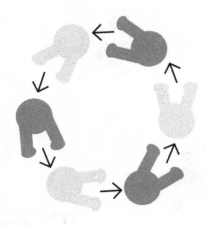

Figure 8: Healing Circle

Cone of Power: One of the most effective techniques for harnessing and directing the raised energy of a group is a cone of power. The cone is directed by one practitioner, while the other participating practitioners power it. The principle is similar to what we've been exploring with the Energy Ring and Wheel and Spokes. As participants channel energy into the center of the circle, the energy will begin to swirl, similarly to how it behaves during the Ring and Wheel exercises. As the energy builds and swirls, a point at the center of the swirl will begin to rise. It's not uncommon to find your hands rising a little with the point of the cone. When the cone gets strong and reaches its peak, the practitioner guiding the cone will shout to release it.

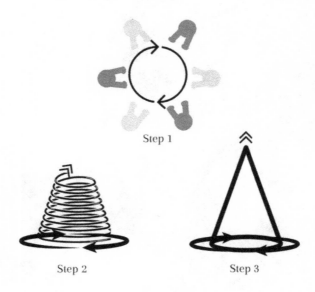

Step 1

Step 2   Step 3

Figure 9: Cone of Power

If you are working with a group, choose a goal for your leader to visualize. This can be the healing of someone who has given consent, or simply the healing of your local environment. It can be happiness or success for your community. Select a goal that has a direct connection to one of the people present.

Your leader will hold the goal of the cone in their mind and focus on the rising point of the cone. When they feel the time is right, they will shout ('now' or 'go' both work well) and visualize the cone reaching its destination.

Chanting as a group is a wonderful way to raise energy for a cone of power. Chants should be simple for group work. For this exercise, please use this one: **Fire and Air, Fire and Air, Earth, Water, Earth, Water**

After your leader has released the cone, ground out any remaining energy by touching the floor. If you would like to practice again so that more than one person is able to try guiding the cone, do so. At the close of this set of exercises, perform your Return to Self Mudra.

Closing the Chapter

If you practiced all or most of the energy work exercises in one session, please perform a thorough grounding and centering (found on page 9). If you have performed any or all of the exercises in this chapter, please eat a snack to help you firmly reintegrate.

Close the Ritual of Study as described on page 36.

CHAPTER THREE HOMEWORK

1. Practice the Blackfeather Self-Blessing, Grounding and Centering, and Shielding daily.
2. Continue memorizing the class ritual opening and closing chants and words.
3. Journaling Exercise: Write down how you are feeling. Notice any areas of fatigue or discomfort and record your mental state. Perform the Energy Body Balancing on page 44. Record your experiences with the exercise. Then, write down a second assessment: how are you feeling after the exercise? Do you notice any differences in how you feel?
4. Journaling Exercise: Perform an energetic evaluation of two different spaces – i.e. a room in your home and the office at work, a restaurant and a doctor's office, or the grocery store and your friend's house. Notice the differences between the two spaces. How do they feel? How do you feel in each of those spaces? When people enter the space, how do they behave?

Chapter 4

Elemental Magick

For this chapter, you will need this book, your Blackfeather oil, your Blackfeather altar, a device that can play a recording online (if so desired), and your journal. This chapter includes a lengthy guided meditation, so a comfortable place to sit where you will be relaxed but not in danger of falling asleep can be useful. This chapter includes both lecture and meditation and should take one to two hours to go through. Your instructor is Irene.

B egin this chapter by performing the opening of the Ritual of Study on page 20.

Magickal Allies

In Western culture, we have behavioral programming around transactional relationships. There is a tendency to have a user attitude as a result: we use stones, plants, products, and even people to achieve our ends because that is considered normal in our culture. Witch-craft, in my personal experience, is more effective when your focus is on building co-creative relationships with spirits, Powers and other Beings.

The discipline of witchcraft suffers from this transactional philoso-phy. We are beginning to change, but a lot of the older texts on correspondences reflect a user-based way of thinking. These texts encourage us to determine the crystals, herbs, elements, and timing needed for a particular piece of spellwork. We are told to obtain those items without giving much thought to where they come from or how that might affect the magick. We're instructed to charge those items with our intent and then use them. Afterward, we are often encouraged to dispose of the spell or ritual remnants by burying them somewhere without consideration for what that might mean for the surrounding flora and fauna.

Shifting our focus toward relationship cultivation and developing spirit allies offers a middle road – a way to access correspondences that is healthier, responsible and respectful. Spells are more effec-tive when the entire team of spirits involved are willing participants as opposed to energetic hostages. Consent is not just good, but vital.

ELEMENTS AND ELEMENTALS

If any class of Being gets referenced more in witchcraft than the Elements, I can't think of it. Even more than the Gods, the Elements or Elementals are Powers we interact with almost constantly and call on in almost every spell and ritual in some way. The Elements we focus on in Blackfeather are Elemental Earth, Air, Fire, Water, and Spirit.

The reason we are focusing on Elementals is that all components of any given spell are under the purview of one of the Elements. For example, if you do not have a relationship with the herb rosemary but you would like to incorporate it into a spell, you can reach that herb through Elemental Earth or Elemental Fire. Both are associated with it. By cultivating a relationship with the Elements you'll be able to connect more easily and in a co-creative way with your spell and ritual components. Think of it as having a mutual friend who can offer a useful introduction.

Spells, rituals, and workings all balance somewhere between the Elements. Some are entirely ruled by one Element, but most incorporate more than one valence or directional pull. Understanding the way the Elements function and the way they balance each other out will help you shape your spells. They're also a useful framework to view many aspects of life through. As we step further and further away from outdated, limiting binary systems, cultivating a set of five polarities helps us describe, access, and relate to different energies. We can describe someone as having fiery personality traits or watery personality traits as opposed to ascribing personality to gender stereotypes.

Meditation and Visualization

People vary in terms of what they experience when they meditate or journey. We use the word visualize, but a better word might be 'imagine.' Not everyone experiences journeys as a visual imagining. If you find that you have problems 'seeing' in your imagination, experiment with tapping into other senses. For some people, the sense of touch or smell is easier to access. When I first began journeying, I had an awareness of what was around me and my sense of touch was pretty accessible, but it took awhile for visuals to become part of my journey experience. If you find that you have better access to awareness of what's around you, touch, scent, or sound, lean into those sensations rather than struggling with trying to "make" yourself "see" something. It's also important to remember that journeying and meditation are skills. They are improved through repetition. Practicing visualization makes us better at it and unfortunately, I have not yet found the substitute for practice.

In my personal experience, the very best way to encounter a noncorporeal being is to journey to meet it. You may have a very real experience by following this journey. You may just get fragments, scents, or sounds. If the following journey proves challenging for you, revisit it as your homework. Remember, that which is fed increases, and a strong imagination is a vital tool for any witch.

This journey includes instructions to make an energetic offering to the beings you will encounter. To do so, simply gather up some of your own energy. Start with an energy ball and then, using visualization, shape it into the form you would like to offer. If you need a refresher on working with energy, revisit Chapter Three.

The early part of this guided journey is based on techniques I learned from Christopher Penczak's Inner Temple of Witchcraft. If you have worked through that book, you may recognize aspects of the early part of this journey. The meditation contained in this chapter is somewhat lengthy and a recording of it is available at blackfeathermystery.com/recordings.

Elemental Meditation

Gently close your eyes or bring them to a half-gaze and allow your breath to deepen and lengthen. Starting at the very top of your head, relax all the muscles around the crown of your head. Allow that feeling of relaxation to spread out and down. Relax your face and jaw, the back of your head, and allow the muscles in your neck to begin relaxing. If it's helpful, feel free to find some little movements to help release tension and find more comfort in your posi-

tion. Continue to feel that wave of relaxation moving through your body. Relax your shoulders, chest and upper back. Relax your mid-back, your belly, and your hips. Relax your legs all the way down to your feet. Relax your arms all the way down to your hands.

Imagine a plain white screen in front of you similar to a projection screen. On that screen, visualize a red number 12. Make it as clear, realistic and distinct as you can. Notice the shade of red and the shape of the numbers.

Visualize an orange number 11. Again, allow this number to become as clear and real as possible.

Visualize a yellow number 10.

See a green number 9 on the screen.

Visualize a blue number 8.

Visualize an indigo number 7 – the color between blue and purple.

Visualize a purple number 6.

Visualize a black number 5.

Visualize a gray number 4.

Visualize a white number 3.

Visualize a silver number 2.

Visualize a clear or crystalline number 1.

Now, I'm going to count down from 13 to one. This time, don't visualize anything, but just let the sound of my voice carry you down (count down from 13 to one).

Visualize your favorite place appearing on the screen in front of you. This is a safe place, a place you can come back to anytime during this meditation. This place is sacred to you, magick in ways only you can understand. Step through the screen and into your favorite place. Look around. Notice what is to your left and right, what is above and below you. Let it become real around you.

A door appears in front of you. This is the Elemental Gate. You can see carvings of crystals, swirls and spirals, flames, waves, and more in the wood of the doorframe. The door itself shimmers a bit with shifting colors. Knowing you are in complete control of everything that happens, reach out and open the door.

A room appears through the doorway. It is circular and there are doors along the wall. Step into the room and close the Elemental Gate behind you. On each door in the circular room is a pentacle. One pentacle is red, one is pale yellow, one is blue, one is green, and one is purple. All are glowing softly. The room is calm and quiet. There is a sense of balance here, and of unchanging peace.

Walk to the door with the red pentacle on it. Again, remembering that you are in control of everything that happens here, reach for the doorknob and open the door.

A gust of hot air greets you. The door opens into a jungle. The sun beats down and vibrant red flowers give off a heady aroma around you. The scent stirs your blood and makes you want to dance or shout. Directly in front of you is a waist-high pillar. Floating over the center of the pillar is a flame. You hear a rumble and look above the tree line. A volcano looms in the distance, sending forth great bursts of flame and magma. You can feel the heat of the volcanic eruption on your face, even at this distance. This is fire in its most primal, powerful form. Independence, determination, and transformation are all qualities of Elemental Fire.

Create an energetic offering to Elemental Fire. It could be a red rose, a shining piece of carnelian, or whatever seems most appropriate to you. Place your offering on the pillar.

On the other side of the pillar, a Fire Elemental begins to take shape. It coalesces from the heat in the air, the fire in the pillar and the volcano in the distance. It is flame embodied. You sense its power, but you do not need to be afraid. Once it has finished forming, the fire Elemental comes closer to the pillar, standing directly across from you.

Respectfully greet the Elemental. Ask them if they are willing to work with you on fire magick.

Ask them what you most need to learn from Elemental Fire right now.

Thank them for their time, and their answers.

The Fire Elemental becomes less distinct, once again dissolving into the land around you. Turn around and walk back through the doorway to the center of the elemental chamber. The door shuts behind you and all is once again quiet.

Walk to the door with the yellow pentacle on it. Again, remembering that you are in control of everything that happens here, reach for the doorknob and open the door.

A sudden gust of wind rushes to meet you. It's cool touch ripples through your hair and swirls around your clothing, carrying with it the scent of springtime. You stand close to the edge of a cliff overlooking a valley. The sun is just cresting the horizon on the far side. The wind rushes toward you from the dawn, blowing back your hair and swirling along the cliff face. You can hear birdsong and other forest chatter within the wind. This is primal air – the wind that whips the waves into a storm and the dawn that breaks through the darkness. Creativity, communication and new beginnings are Elemental Air's provenance.

Create an energetic offering to Elemental Air. It could be a feather, a fragrant flower, incense, or whatever seems most appropriate to you. Place your offering at the edge of the cliff.

The wind strengthens and seems to whirl in front of you in a spiral. An Air Elemental begins to take shape. It shapes itself out of the dawn sunlight, the winds and the scents, songs, and stories that are carried on the breeze. Once it has finished forming, the Air Elemental drifts closer to you.

Respectfully greet the Elemental. Ask them if they are willing to work with you on air magick.

Ask them what you most need to learn from Elemental Air right now.

Thank them for their time, and their answers.

The Air Elemental becomes less distinct, once again dissolving into the land around you. You look out across the valley one last time, then turn and walk back through the doorway to the center of the elemental chamber. The door shuts behind you and all is once again quiet.

Walk to the door with the blue pentacle on it. Again, remembering that you are in control of everything that happens here, reach for the doorknob and open the door.

You smell the salt air as the door reveals the crashing waves and white sand of a vast shoreline. The sun is setting off to the west amidst growing thunderheads. You move forward and feel the wet sand on the soles of your feet. The crashing waves kick up spray that gently mists your skin and clothing with a fine layer of moisture. You hear a rumbling from the sky and look up...just as the heavens unleash a torrent of rain. You throw your arms wide to the warm rain as the waves reach further up the shore to touch your feet. This is primal water – the living element – emotions and love reside in water's fluid sphere. Elemental Water governs compassion for others and ourselves, intuition and dreams.

Create an energetic offering to Elemental Water. It could be a blue stone, a seashell, or whatever seems most appropriate to you. Place your offering on the sand.

The ocean begins to swell and bubble in front of you and the rain grows stronger. A Water Elemental begins to take shape. It grows out of the waters around you – the sea spray, the rain and the ocean itself. Once it has finished forming, the Water Elemental washes closer to you.

Respectfully greet the Elemental. Ask them if they are willing to work with you on water magick.

Ask them what you most need to learn from Elemental Water right now.

Thank them for their time, and their answers.

The Water Elemental begins to dissipate, dissolving into the air and sea. You look across the storm-tossed ocean one last time, then turn and walk back through the doorway to the center of the elemental chamber. The door shuts behind you and all is once again quiet.

Walk to the door with the green pentacle on it. Again, remembering that you are in control of everything that happens here, reach for the doorknob and open the door.

The scent of pine greets you as you open the door to a forest at night. The trees are huge, stretching high above you, swaying in the gentle breeze. A bright full moon beams down, illuminating the woods around you. You are standing on the foothills of a mountain. As you look past the trees, you can see the moonlit snow-capped peaks gleaming in the distance. You walk to the nearest tree, an oak, and place your hands upon its bark. The texture is rough yet pleasant to touch and you can feel a subtle energy within the tree, coursing through the bark beneath your fingertips. There is a sense of timelessness around you – this forest was here before your birth and will be here after you move on to the next life. This is primal earth – stability, death, rebirth, and manifestation are Earth's provenance.

Create an energetic offering to Elemental Earth. It could be a crystal, a pine cone, a seedling or whatever seems most appropriate to you. Place your offering on the forest floor.

From the shadows of the forest, an Earth Elemental begins to take shape. It grows out of the mossy stones, the crumbling black earth and the green life surrounding you. You sense its power, but you do not need to be afraid. Once it has finished forming, the Earth Elemental walks toward you, heavy footsteps muffled by the pine needles on the forest floor.

Respectfully greet the Elemental.
Ask them if they are willing to work with you on earth
magick.
Ask them what you most need to learn from Elemental Earth
right now.
Thank them for their time, and their answers.

The Earth Elemental begins to tumble apart, returning to the stones, leaves and dirt that it was made of. You bid the night forest farewell, then turn and walk back through the doorway to the center of the elemental chamber. The door shuts behind you and all is once again quiet.

Walk to the door with the purple pentacle on it. Again, remembering that you are in control of everything that happens here, reach for the doorknob and open the door.

You hear the sound of a deep chime ringing as you throw open the door to the vast expanse of space. Infinity stretches away in every direction. Galaxies whirl in their starry sphere...suns, moons, and planets dancing the dance of eternity. This is the realm of Spirit. The energy of all life is present here, reverberating around you, reaching out to embrace you in welcome. It is the element of Spirit that holds all the other elements together. Spirit is in everything. Spirit is everything.

Create an energetic offering to Elemental Spirit. It could be a swirling spiral, a white lotus, a spark of starlight, or whatever seems most appropriate to you. Release your offering into the Universe.

Starlight and dark matter begin to ripple in front of you. A Spirit Elemental is taking shape. It forms itself out of the light, the dark, and the raw ingredients for life. You sense its power, but you do not need to be afraid. Once it has finished forming, the Spirit Elemental drifts toward you.

> *Respectfully greet the Elemental. Ask them if they are willing to work with you on spirit magick.*
> *Ask them what you most need to learn from Elemental Spirit right now.*
> *Thank them for their time, and their answers.*

The spirit Elemental begins to drift apart, light and darkness rippling back out into eternity. You gaze upon the starry expanse once more, then close the door and walk back to the center of the elemental chamber.

Look around the chamber. Mark it in your memory so that you can return here whenever you need to.

Begin to deepen and lengthen your breath. Wiggle your fingers and toes, roll your shoulders, gently shift around. Reconnect to your body, to this space, to this time. Take a deep breath in. Let it out on a sigh. Whenever you are ready, gently open your eyes.

Reflections

In your journal, record your experience with this journey. Write down the messages from each elemental you spoke with. Then, answer these questions:

What element do you feel closest to?

What element do you have the hardest time connecting to?

Take a moment to consider what you are working on in your life right now and where it fits in relationship to the Elements. This doesn't have to be an overtly metaphysical goal – practical considerations are also ruled by Elements. In your journal, write down which Elements are most prominent in your life at the moment.

When you have finished your session, close the Ritual of Study as described on page 36.

CHAPTER FOUR HOMEWORK

1. Practice the Blackfeather Self-Blessing, Grounding and Centering, and Shielding daily.
2. Continue memorizing the class ritual, opening and closing chants and words.
3. Journaling Exercise: Explore your personality using the elements as the anchor points you balance between. Do you have a dominant element or elements? Do you feel like you would benefit from more or less of any particular element in your life?

CHAPTER 5

THE WITCH'S CUPBOARD

For this chapter, you will need this book, your Blackfeather oil, your Blackfeather altar, a device that can play a recording online (if so desired), and your journal. This chapter is lecture-based, and should take one to two hours to go through. Your instructor is Irene.

B egin this chapter by performing the opening of the Ritual of Study on page 20.

Although Blackfeather Mystery School focuses primarily on cocreative, relationship-based magick, there are some items, practices, enchantments and recipes that are really, REALLY useful to have on hand. We don't always have time to go find a spirit ally and cultivate a relationship when things get scary. Sometimes the best solution is still black salt and a witch bottle.

This class is going to cover the items I maintain in my own magickal cupboard as well as how to create and/or use them. I tend toward a minimalist philosophy of life, so you won't be terribly surprised to hear that my magickal cupboard does not include a small bottle of every herb carried at my local witch shop. I keep the supplies on hand that I use most frequently. I maintain the spells and enchantments that have been most useful to me. Witches, as we often say, are practical people.

APOTROPAICS

Apotropaics are objects and practices attributed with the power to avert misfortune. The most common examples of this in our culture is saying 'bless you' when someone sneezes, carrying a 'lucky' object of some sort and knocking on wood when discussing something that could go wrong. These are all low-level apotropaics and are so common that we really don't think about them very much anymore. A witch's cupboard contains much stronger apotropaics. There are a few reasons for this.

One of the downsides of openly practicing witchcraft is that people with a dislike of magick will sometimes take issue with your life path. This can take many forms – it can be overt or subtle. Overt rejection is sometimes easier to deal with simply because then at least you know where you stand. Subtle disapproval is more common in friendships and familial relationships. When you tell people what you are doing, sometimes they choose (consciously or unconsciously) to work against you. This is also true on a larger scale. Sadly, even to this day, witches, pagans, and other magickal folk are frequently viewed with skepticism, disapproval and alarm. When that is the case, the thoughts and energy of the disapproving party may be focused on doing a witch ill. Hoping for ill luck to befall someone is one of the sources of 'evil eye' style curses.

Witches are also frequently the target of jealousy. Out of all the human emotions, jealousy is one of the most destructive and is *also* frequently at the root of 'evil eye' curses. When you stand in your strength, in your empowerment, in your truth, people who have not made the personal journey to claim their sovereignty can be jealous. They may envy your ability to move through the world in a way they feel they cannot. If you are physically attractive within the parameters of your cultural standards, the risk is even higher.

Lastly, witches frequently end up in situations that require the use of strong apotropaics. We are natural helpers. Most of us get into witchcraft because we want to help heal the world and the people in it. This means that we are often sought out by people who are in desperate situations: they are the subject of strong hexes or curses themselves, they are actively attracting harmful spirits and energies, or they are in emotional/psychological free fall. All of those situations can easily bleed energy and influence onto the witch trying to help the distressed individual. We are also regularly called upon to assist with places that are the subject of energetic or spirit-linked, discordant energy.

All of this means that maintaining a collection of strong hex breaking objects and enchantments is vital to our work. Most witches have heavily shielded and enchanted houses for good reason.

Recommended Apotropaics

Black Salt: I go through this in large quantities. Black salt is simply normal salt mixed with fine ashes from the fire pit. Ashes from magickal fires can add some juice to black salt. One of my friends makes their year's supply using the ashes from the Yule fire. To make your own, mix two parts salt (sea or fine ground - it doesn't really matter) to one part ashes. Black salt is also commercially available at your local witch store.

Black salt is a strong boundary-setting substance. I regularly run a line of black salt along all the outward-facing walls, windows and thresholds of my home. I also run a line along the outside wall of the house, and along the entire border of my property. It's probably overkill, but I'm an out, publicly known witch. It comes with occupational hazards.

When we are asleep, we are at our most vulnerable. For that reason, I also sprinkle black salt between the box spring and mattress of my bed. It keeps nightmares down, limiting them to ones that are the product of my own mind rather than external sources.

When I am doing work that involves hex breaking or deep energy work, I run a line of black salt around my work space. Hexes don't want to be broken. Their originators don't want you to destroy them. Depending on the strength of the hex, it will sometimes try to stop you. One very large hex breaking for an extraordinarily nasty curse springs to mind as an example. During the course of that day, my normally reliable printer went down while printing materials for the ceremony. Multiple people involved in the ceremony experienced car trouble, heavy traffic at odd hours, or had their navigators go haywire causing them to almost miss the ceremony. The entire day was studded with things screwing up. The hex knew we were coming for it and tried to fight back.

This can occur on a smaller scale. Moreover, while a witch or spirit worker is engaged in healing work, their client's energy field and sometimes their own is a little more vulnerable than usual. A ring of black salt contains the energies you are working with and keeps malicious energies out.

Black salt is also frequently used as an ingredient in protective spells like pouches, sachets and witch bottles (more on that later). I consider it a vital component of my cupboard.

To dispose of black salt after use, simply sweep it up with a brush and dustpan, or vacuum it up and throw it away. Remember that salt has a dampening effect on the fertility of any land it comes in contact with – be careful when using it outdoors.

Frankincense oil, resin and quick-light charcoal: Frankincense is one of the strongest anti-bad-shit substances out there. In both oil and resin form, it's incredibly powerful for banishing discordant, malicious, or harmful energies and spirits. My cabinet includes both oil and resin, and a few small cast iron cauldrons for smoldering the resin in. The smoke from frankincense resin is very strong and thick – make sure to crack a window if you are using it indoors.

Frankincense is my go-to when smoldering other incense hasn't worked. Sage is commonly used as a clearing, purifying incense. If you are using sage, please use a variety that is not part of a closed tradition or closed practice. For example, the use of white sage for purification by individuals who are not members of a First Nations tribe is culturally appropriative. I use broadleaf sage personally, but there are many varieties available. However, some energies are just too entrenched or too strong for sage. When that is the case, I use frankincense smoke instead. To cleanse an area or object using frankincense smoke, get an instant-light charcoal going strongly in a heat resistant container. I like to use small cast iron cauldrons for this. Sprinkle the resin on the charcoal. As it melts, it will begin to release smoke. You can then pass objects through the smoke or carry the cauldron around (by the handle – they get HOT, you may need oven mitts) to waft smoke throughout a space or around a person. Make sure you open a window – the smoke from resins like frankincense can cause irritation.

Frankincense oil can be used to anoint people, doorways, windows and anything else you want to either remove invasive energy from or protect. When I reset the wards on my house (I do this twice yearly), anointing the doors and windows with frankincense oil is part of the magickal protocol I follow.

One note about Frankincense: this is an overharvested resin, which means we need to source our supplies from ethical merchants and use them sparingly.

Iron: The folklore from vastly different parts of the world attributes the same magickal properties to iron – it is widely used to repel spirits and energy. The only problem is that iron tends to repel ALL spirits and not just malevolent ones. As a result, depending on the pantheon or spirits you work with, iron may not be an appropriate tool. Some land spirits find it offensive as do many fae beings.

Spikes and nails: Railroad spikes can be pounded into the earth to help create a boundary around a house or specific location (again, talk to your land spirits before you do this). Iron nails are used for the same purpose and also as ingredients in witch bottles and some protective spells.

Filings: Iron filings (tiny fragments of iron left over from the black-smithing process/grinding) are most commonly used to 'feed' lode-stones in prosperity-drawing magick but can also be used as a repelling component in sachets or bottles. The presence of a magnetic force changes them from repelling to drawing energy.

Blades: A cold iron blade is a wonderfully useful tool for cutting energetic connections. Energy cords or connections form between people as their emotional closeness grows. This is part of why your best friend will call at exactly the right moment, or why a parent will psychically know when their child is in trouble. These cords are beautiful connections in healthy relationships. However, cords can also form between abusers and victims, energy vampires and prey, and can also remain after a relationship turns sour. Using a cold iron blade to cut those energetic connections is quite effective.

To perform cord cutting with a blade, create sacred, protected space. Then, concentrate on the bond between you and the individual you are connected to. Tune in to your body and notice where you physically feel pressure/connection the most. The heart is common, but we also can have cords attached to our heads, genitals, bellies, and backs. When you have determined where the cord is attached to you, fill the blade with your intention of severing the connection. Then, slowly run the blade over that part of your body, just above the skin. This may require the assistance of a partner depending on where the cord is attached.

Notice how you feel as the blade passes. It may take a couple passes over a connection to sever the cord. Cords we are involuntarily connected to may take more than one session to fully remove. When the individual on the other end of the cord senses your detachment from them, they will frequently try to reconnect the cord. Be aware of this potential and plan to set firm boundaries if they contact you.

Witch bottles: A witch bottle is a magickal device used to repel malicious/malevolent energies, spirits, and individuals. Witch bottles have been in use since the 16th century at least and exist to this day for good reason – they are quite effective. To create a witch bottle, simply fill a bottle with a cork, cap or top with repellent ingredients: iron nails, cat's claws, iron filings, broken glass, frankincense resin, small stones with protective qualities, toxic, poisonous or discomfort-inducing substances and other material both magickal and mundane that have a 'get the fuck away from me' quality. Then, add some of your own urine. Seal the bottle and melt wax (I like to use black or red candle wax) over the top of the bottle to seal it. You can bury the bottle at the edge of your property, hide it in the attic, tuck it inside a wall during renovation or otherwise place it somewhere toward the edge of the area you wish to shield where it won't be disturbed. I consider witch bottles to be fundamental components of a ward system for any dwelling.

Protective stones: Begin a relationship with a stone associated with protection. I work most closely with black tourmaline, but most dark-colored stones have protective properties. This applies to stones found locally as well as to specific varieties listed in stone correspondences. Maintain a good handful or so of these stones. They are wonderfully useful for setting space. If you are staying in a place that is not your home, you can place them around the perimeter of the room to hold an energetic boundary. They can be used to boost your wards in your home. You can include them in circle casting when you're doing any kind of magick that might leave you or other participants vulnerable. They're just a super useful tool to have on hand.

General protective/purification incense: During a working, it is good to have a smoldering herb or resin compound with which to purify the air with smoke. There are dozens of possibilities here for herbs and herbal blends. I grow broad leafed garden sage, patchouli, and lavender and make herb bundles from the combination of them every year and they are what I use for this purpose. However, stick, cone and loose-leaf incense is also an option. There are many commercially available blends specifically for protection. Most sharp-scented herbs and spices have protective properties. In a pinch, raid your spice cabinet – cinnamon, clove, rosemary, bay, black pepper, dill, and cumin can all be used. For more information on protective herbs, I recommend Cunningham's Encyclopedia of Magickal Herbs by Scott Cunningham. For information specifically about purification and protection via smoldering herbs, I recommend Sacred Smoke by Amy Blackthorn.

HEALING

The other service witches are frequently called upon to assist with is healing. We are regularly asked to light candles, send energy or perform healing spells and ceremonies for people, spirits, ancestors and even pets.

Candles: Keep a supply of candles in healing colors of a couple different sizes. Colors associated with healing are white, silver and most shades of blue and green. I like to keep some small candles on hand for magick that needs to be directed during a specific and small window of time. For example, when a friend is going in for a short medical procedure, a candle that burns for that specific window of time is more useful than a large candle designed to burn for several days. For longer-term healing and energy-sending, I use tall, unscented jar candles available at most bodegas and witch stores. They can be burned for many days in a row and have the added benefit of being in a heat resistant holder, so there's less risk of fire if they are left unattended. Not that you should do that, but accidents happen.

Minerals: Crystal therapy – the use of gems, minerals and metals to heal or create change – is an utterly massive field within witchcraft and can become an immersive area of study. If the use of crystals resonates with you, I do encourage you to explore that path. For those of us who are less oriented toward that focus, a simple selection of healing stones is useful to have on hand. I recommend keeping a 'chakra set,' a collection of seven stones attuned to each chakra in the human body. These sets can be purchased or can be generated cooperatively with our local land spirits.

To use a chakra stone, first determine the chakra most closely tied to the current illness. For example, fertility problems are most closely related to the sacral chakra. Emotional pain is most closely linked to the heart chakra. Once you have selected the correct stone, fill it with energy and intent. Revisit Raising Energy in Chapter Three if you need a refresher on ways to do so. The charged stone can then be placed on the person you are healing or incorporated into a spell you are working on.

Healing magick is an entire field within witchcraft that includes a lot of different techniques. Simple healing magick, like charging a stone, is just the tip of the iceberg. Most importantly, whenever performing healing for others, obtain consent from the person you are helping. We will be covering more healing techniques later in this book.

I also recommend that you keep a handful of single-termination quartz crystal points. They are useful for charging with energy and intent and then incorporating into spells, rituals, and other workings.

If you choose to purchase crystals, stones, or other minerals, seek out ethically mined or collected crystals. The gemstone industry has historically been plagued with pollution, dangerous working conditions, low wages for workers, and other problematic practices. We want our stone allies to come to us healthy and free of harmful influences. There are vendors that specifically offer ethically sourced crystals online. Moreover, many smaller vendors like your local New Age or Metaphysical store can tell you where their stones come from. Always learn the origin of a stone before you purchase it.

GENERAL SPELLCRAFT

Healing and Hex-removing/Protection are far from the only options when it comes to magickal work. Having a decent selection of multifaceted tools on hand can help support spellcraft and charm work.

Candles: Candles are one of the most common components of a spell. I like to keep a few candles in each of the primary and secondary colors, gold, silver, black and white. As with the candles listed in healing supplies, a couple of different sizes are useful. Small tapers that burn down in under an hour and birthday cake candles are useful for spells that are specific to a window of time, or that require the candle to burn out completely. Jar prayer candles are available in most colors and are good for spells requiring longer term burning.

Incense: Incense is useful for many things – setting a mood, tapping into a specific energy, clearing energy, blessing, burning as offerings and more. If there are specific incense types that the pantheon or spirits you work with like, keep those in your collection as well (for example, I always have amber incense on hand for working with the Norse goddess Freya). I like to keep a selection of bright or solar incense, protective incense (usually resin based), and an incense associated with spiritual connection on hand at a minimum.

Minerals: Along with a set of healing stones, consider keeping a few other kinds of stones on hand.

Grounding: Stones that help earth energy, or that can be used to pour excess energy into. I like rough, dark-colored stones for general grounding. These are useful for placing around the house during gatherings of people as a general earthing grid. For individual grounding, there's nothing quite like a big, smooth river rock. After a lot of journey or ritual work, I like to sit with a heavy stone on my lap to help me reintegrate and get stable and centered in my body again. If I'm experiencing an overabundance of a particular emotion or energy, a large stone can serve as a good receptacle for that overflow.

Attracting: Lodestones or magnetized stones are most frequently used to attract wealth, but they can be charged to attract many things.

Fabric and string: Many spells involve sachets, spirit bags and other fabric-wrapped collections of items. Having a neutral-colored fabric on hand and some yarn, jute or sewing floss makes creating these easier. At most fabric stores, there's a 'remnants' pile with small quantities of marked-down fabric in it. I generally source my fabric there or I recycle clothing that I have worn through. If you need a larger quantity of fabric, I recommend hitting your local Goodwill or thrift store. They carry inexpensive textiles (sheets, curtains, blankets, tablecloths) and can be a great source for both upcycling and not breaking the bank. If the sachet you are making needs to be burned or buried at any point, make sure that the fabric is linen, 100% cotton, bamboo or another natural fiber that will biodegrade or burn without releasing any harmful substances into the air or earth.

Paper: Many spells also involve writing things on paper and then burning it, storing it somehow or burying it. Purchasing or making herbal paper can be a wonderful way to incorporate a little more magick into this practice (although the paper you have at home will also work). There are simple instructions for making herbal paper available online, generally using recycled paper or newsprint and dried herbs. Again, if your paper is going to be burned, pay attention to what it is made out of. Try to use recycled, unbleached paper when possible.

Oils: Oils are frequently used as ingredients for various spells – they are rubbed on candles, dripped onto stones, mixed in with herbs, burned as part of incense, used to anoint our bodies, etc. This particular collection will evolve as you practice. I have about ten essential oils I regularly use that range from protective to enhancing of spiritual connection. Oil use can become a huge area of focus, although that particular part of magick can become a bit risky in terms of being taken advantage of. There are quite a few pyramid scheme 'businesses' involved with selling oils. Try to use essential oils with safe base carriers like almond oil. Also, remember that your preferences matter. I find most blessing oil mixes to be too floral for my taste. Part of why my oils collection is fairly small is my pickiness about scent. The good news is that if you are also fairly choosy, almost any magickal goal you are pursuing can be supported by a few different oils. Choose the ones that work for you.

DIVINATION

Divinatory tools are used for so much more than simply doing readings for others (although that's awesome too). In spellcraft, consult your divinatory tool to help determine the best path forward and to identify potential obstacles. Tools like tarot, runes, and ogham (the Celtic tree-based divination system) can often be used as part of spells. Divinatory tools can also be used after performing a spell to check on its efficacy and see whether any additional work is needed. A divinatory tool that gives more than a yes, no, or maybe answer is most useful in spellcraft. Pendulums and dowsing rods are wonderful for detecting energy and answering simple questions, but they are less able to convey nuance.

Choose a divinatory tool you feel drawn to, even if the reasons are unclear to you. The attraction we feel to our tools is vital: we are more likely to work with tools we adore. Once you have chosen a tool (a tarot or oracle card deck, a rune or ogham set, I Ching or Kahina stones – there are so many options), perform a simple tool consecration.

To do so, place a bowl of finely ground salt, a white candle in a holder, and your divinatory tool on your altar. Create sacred space in the same way that you open your study sessions. Sprinkle a little bit of salt on your divinatory tool to release any discordant energy it may be carrying. Then, pass your divinatory tool above the flame of the candle and say, or silently think, the words of the consecration.

> **By the bright flame of knowledge, the fire of the stars,**
> **I bless this/these _____ and consecrate it/them**
> **to the sacred purpose of Clarity.**
> **By the Powers above, below and within, so may it be!**

Sit with your divinatory tool and explore it. Look at the cards or sigils. Get a feel for its energy and share your own with it. Write down your initial impressions in your journal. Then, snuff the candle and close the ritual in the same way you close your study sessions.

If you are just learning your divination system, add a daily draw to your Blackfeather practice. This is *not* meant to be a divination for the day – it is simply a way to learn your system. Every day, draw one or two cards/runes/stones/etc and meditate on their meaning. This will help you commit them to memory.

STORAGE

Although most of us would like a proper Witch's Cupboard some-where in the house, it's not always practical or affordable to find our perfect Cupboard. I personally use lidded, latchable plastic bins. These keep dust and cat fur out and off of things and are also easy to label. Moreover, if small hands or curious felines are a concern in your house, small latching bins can be stored out of reach and look a good deal less interesting to kids than a cupboard living in plain sight. You can repurpose existing furniture as well – a small dresser or chest of drawers can make a wonderful Cupboard.

To keep dried herbs fresh and potent the longest, try to store them in small, airtight containers. Upcycling your spice jars once they run out can be a good way to do this. Oils and candles should be stored out of direct sunlight – they can both be damaged by excessive light for different reasons.

Maintain an awareness of the nature of the different objects you are storing. Try not to store your apotropaics (especially things like iron nails) directly alongside items related to spiritual connection or communication.

One of my favorite Alton Brown quotes is 'Organization will set you free.' Part of how that manifests in my own cupboard is through 'kits.' I have a 'Go Bag.' It's an entire kit of apotropaics – when shit gets real, I just grab the bag and know everything I need is inside it. I also have a healing kit that goes with me to my spirit working sessions. It contains everything I need for a session all in one place. If you find you are doing specific kinds of work regularly (purification, healing, protection, hex removal), consider grouping those items in a smaller bag or container that's easy to grab. It saves time when you need a particular collection of tools. Remember to package your tools safely – wrapping divinatory tools or anything sharp in fabric, cases, and holders is a good idea.

Close the Ritual of Study as described on page 36.

CHAPTER FIVE HOMEWORK

1. Practice the Blackfeather Self-Blessing, Grounding and Centering, and Shielding daily.
2. Continue memorizing the class ritual, opening and closing chants and words.
3. Begin gathering supplies for your witch's cupboard. Remember that you do not need to gather them all at once or spend outside your ability level. Found, previously owned, and thrifted items work perfectly well. If you *are* purchasing new supplies, try to support your local witch store.
4. Select a divinatory tool and consecrate it. Add a short divinatory practice to your daily practice, drawing one or two stones/cards/etc, and looking up the meanings of them. Remember, this is not a divination for the day. It is simply a way to help learn your divinatory tool's language.

CHAPTER 6

MAGICKAL SELF DEFENSE

*For this chapter, you will need this book, your Blackfeather
oil, your Blackfeather altar, a device that can play a
recording online (if so desired), your journal, and a partner
if you are working with one. All exercises can also be
performed solitary. This chapter is lecture-based with two
small exercises, and should take two to three hours to go
through. Your instructor is Irene.*

B egin this chapter by performing the opening of the Ritual of
Study on page 20.

POWER

Magickal people – witches, magicians, spirit workers and the like –
are a bit like the flames of candles in a dark room. If we think of
magickal skill as being at the core of the 'flame,' magickal folk
shine very brightly. That brightness draws things to us. Some of

those things are good – sometimes it's other bright "lights," or helpful spirits, or Gods. However, we also draw "moths." Those moths can take multiple forms. The most common, of course, is other humans who have low energy and therefore need to absorb energy from others. With some people this behavior is pretty mild – the person in question has a bad day and needs to vent and feels buoyed up after the conversation since they were able to absorb some of your attention – your energy. This same person on a different day will have enough of their own reserves not to feed off yours, or even to offer you energy if you're having a bad day. At the other end of the spectrum is an energy vampire. Energy vampires are corporeal humans who are unable to generate enough natural energy of their own and consistently need to absorb energy from other people. After interacting with an uncontrolled energy vampire, you will feel drained or listless even if you normally love being around other people.

Along with human "moths," there are other beings that can be a threat to people who shine. Our world is shared by many noncorporeal and incorporeal spirits. Some of them will try to attach to a bright spirit in an attempt to prolong their existence. This is especially true of shells – pieces of an individual's energy body/ego that did not unspool correctly when they died. Malicious land spirits, demons and deities – noncorporeal beings – are rarer than people tend to think. In the vast majority of cases, a nonphysical being attempting to feed off of or cause harm to someone is the leftover bits of a dead human.

One of the other problems of being energetically highly visible – a flame in a dark room – is that brightness can draw the attention of people who are psychologically imbalanced. I don't love the histrionics frequently associated with the concept of psychic attack, but it definitely exists. Many times, the ill intention directed toward the victim is not conscious. The number of people I know who have been the targets of a deliberate curse or baneful hex is very, very small. MOST of the time, when we're talking about psychic attack, we're talking about someone sending generalized bad vibes out of anger/frustration with or hatred/jealousy of the victim. Unfortunately, if you're doing anything worth doing, *somebody* will take it the wrong way.

Just to make things extra fun, there's an additional layer that can impact magickal folk – many of us (though by no means all) are empathic or psychic. This means we easily take on the thoughts and emotions of others and experience them as though they are our own. This is an exhausting way to live. It's also very difficult to separate out our own emotions and instincts when they are drowned out by a cacophony of other thoughts.

All of this is to say that the art of magickal self-defense is one of the most important tools a witch can have in their toolbox. As witches, we must own our power – that means taking sovereignty of and responsibility for it. Unguarded energy and life force is effectively adrift and can be used, manipulated, stolen or just siphoned off by day to day interactions with people.

SHIELDING

Energy Exercise

This exercise works best with a partner. If you are able to practice with someone else, please do so. Otherwise, simply read through this section for later reference.

Becoming master of and responsible for your power starts at the center first – it starts with you.

To do this shielding exercise, stand facing your partner, far enough away that one of you can fully extend your arms without touching the other. Please be careful – if either of you feels like you are going to fall at any point in time, stop the exercise.

> One at a time, using only energy channeled through your hands, try to push your partner.

> Then, again using only energy, try to pull your partner toward you. When you have finished, switch places.

> Give each other some feedback about what you observed.

> Now, raise your shields.

Perform the same exercise again. One at a time, try to push your partner, then pull them. When you have finished, switch places.

Give each other some feedback again. What was different this time?

Impermeable, Semipermeable and Specific Permeability

The very first chapter of this book taught you a shielding practice to begin using daily. It's a basic impermeable shield that is sourced from the life force/prana/chi/ki that holds our world together. In an ideal world, we shield ourselves first thing in the morning, again at midday and possibly once more in the evening depending on our schedules and home life. Part of getting into a habit with raising your shields every day is so that they are in place should you need them. Remember that shields are a proactive measure – they don't work as effectively in retrospect.

As we move through the world, creating and maintaining a few different shields can be very useful. Impermeable shields are great for being out and about, but what about situations where you *do* want to be aware of the psychic energy around you? Or situations where you need to be open to specific people but not open to others?

Impermeable shields These shields block everything – good intentions and ill – from all beings and spaces. Some people include a bounce-back on their impermeable shields – an automated response to an attempt to influence the wearer. One of my dearest friends wears a Rue shield – Rue frequently causes blistering in anyone who touches it. My own impermeable shield, and the one taught in chapter 1, is made of green flame. It doesn't have a bounce-back, but if someone touches it long enough, they get burned.

Semi-permeable: These shields allow specific types of energy in. They're targeted for ill-intent but allow psychic input from beings and spaces that are not malevolent. These are useful for shared spaces where you do wish to connect with others. I use semi-permeable shields for leading rituals, presenting workshops and teaching yoga. I need to be able to read the psychic pulse of a room and feel available to my students.

Specific-permeability: This kind of shield is open to specific individuals (rather than types of energy). I find having a specific-permeability shield to be useful since I am frequently in the company of my partner, or of the members of my band, but *also* in a busy environment. It allows me to choose who I am open to, and who can 'hear' me.

You already know one impermeable shield well, so working on a semi-permeable or specific shield comes next.

Creating Your Shield(s)

Once you have selected the kind of shield you wish to create, choose a visualization for that shield. I suggest selecting one that's easy to summon. I use green fire, mirrors, crystals, stones and earth formations for mine because I can visualize those substances easily.

A semi-permeable shield could be a visualization that is translucent or semitransparent. I find that visualizing a translucent crystal barrier works well here. Quartz (smoky or occluded), Amethyst, Citrine, Opal, Fluorite, and Diamond (occluded) are all good options. To create a specific-permeability shield, you will need to visualize access points for the individuals you wish to be open to as part of the shield.

Decide how the shield will be powered. All shields (all spells, all energetic structures) require some sort of power source. The stronger the power source, the stronger the shield. Most of us use a little of our own energy (prana, chi, or ki) to set a shield. We feed energy to the shield as we visualize it forming around us. As you already know from your shielding visualization, you can also use the energy field around us. In magick, the most common ways to raise energy are to chant or sing, dance, or perform breathing exercises. This form of power raising can be too time-consuming for daily use, but if you link your shield to a particular talisman or piece of jewelry, you can use that technique to power it.

To create a talisman-anchored shield, raise energy in the way you prefer, then direct it and your shield visualization into your talisman. When you wear or carry that talisman going forward, the shields attached to it are very strong. However, stored energy decreases with use. Remember that you will need to periodically recharge the talisman. How often depends on how much use your shields see.

Once you have created a set of shields, practice using them – raising and lowering them – until they can go up almost instantaneously. As with all things magick, that which is fed increases. Becoming good at shielding and defensive magick means practicing it.

If you wrestle with anxiety or depression, including a 'drain' in your shield can be useful for siphoning off your own anxious energy. You can also release that energy by grounding and centering after removing your shield at home at the end of the day.

WARDING

Creating a safe space in which to relax and let down our guard is the focus of a lot of house and hearth magick. Some of the oldest charms and magickal devices our archeologists find are specifically for protecting one's home, property and lands. We can draw inspiration and ideas from these practices, many of which are being revisited and revised to this day. Witch bottles, incantation bowls and all manner of ancient protection magick still work. We also have some newer magickal tech to choose from, not to mention the protective possibilities that occur when cultivating a co-creative relationship with land, familial and house spirits.

There's a well-deserved link described between witches and their houses in folklore. The old stories tell us about witches who live in magickal homes made of bones, herbs, candy, or all manner of other things. Those homes contain magickal objects and frequently are at the center of a witch's abilities. Along with being a safe space, *a witch's home can be a source of power*. Most of us do the bulk of our magick inside our homes.

Basic Home Warding

Begin by introducing yourself to your house or apartment. My preferred way to do this is to sit on the floor with both hands touching the floor, or to stand with one hand touching the wall. I then gently soften my shields (I wear a set that includes psychic 'blinders' so that I don't get distracted by all the energetic noise around me) and reach out to the spirit of the house or apartment. Almost all dwelling places have an egregore – an energy body. The egregore generally takes on much of the character of the emotions frequently experienced within the home and they usually adapt to match different human caretakers over the course of time.

When you feel that gentle sense of presence responding to your query, introduce yourself if you haven't done so before. You can do this aloud or silently. Explain your intentions – that you want to help protect the home (and land, if applicable) from ill will and malicious energy. Try to obtain some indication of consent from the egregore. Most are happy to have some help.

Raise energy to begin generating the shield. You can chant, dance, drum, rattle...there are lots of possibilities. Revisit chapter three if you need some ideas. I like to chant because it leaves my hands free to help shape the energy structure I'm forming. Begin by visualizing a sphere forming in front of you that's roughly the size of a beach ball. That sphere is going to end up being the shield, but we start small to establish the character of it. Design your shield as you see fit. For example, you can visualize it as having a mirrored surface to bounce back any energy directed at it. If you live in an area with a lot of crime, you can add some spikes to the outside of the shield to make your home unattractive as a target. Other visualizations include stone, metal, castle walls, flames....each shield has its own character.

Once you've established a firm visualization for your shield, begin to 'inflate' it. Pour the energy you're raising into that sphere and watch it expand. Allow it to fill the room, then expand past it, leaving you inside. Expand the shield until it's large enough to encompass the house or apartment you're shielding. Then, settle the shield into place, visualizing it centering perfectly around your home. Once it is positioned, "thicken" the shield. Pour more energy and visualization into it until the shield walls are dense and firmly set.

Check in with the egregore of the home again before you conclude your work just to make sure it's comfortable with the shield. Listen for any suggestions or feedback.

When a shield is constructed of raised energy, it is necessary to replenish the shield every few months. Remember that energy dissipates naturally. Shields also need to be boosted if they're bouncing back a lot of energy or deterring beings from approaching your property. The energy used for those purposes will need to be refreshed.

There are ways to make a shield longer-lasting and stronger, but they take a little more work and preparation. One of my favorite ways to boost a shield is to use anchor stones. Anchor stones help ground your shield and feed it additional energy. They can also act as repellants themselves depending on the kind of stone and any sigils or symbols you etch onto them.

My preference for anchor stones is to use stones that are already part of the environment around the home. Another option is to choose stones that are associated with protection metaphysically. Most of the darker, heavier stones have this association. One of my favorite crystals for this purpose is black tourmaline. It'll ground damn near anything. Jet, Obsidian, Hematite, black Kyanite and Onyx can also be used.

Before you create your shield, cleanse the stones you choose to use. There are many options for cleansing. You can place the stones in a bowl of salt overnight, put them on the ground in bright sunlight all day or thoroughly waft a purifying incense over them. One lovely way to cleanse stones involves running water. If you are lucky enough to live near a stream or river, you can place your stones in a mesh or fabric bag and put them somewhere the current will wash over them for a day.

Then, wake up your stones. My preferred method is to gently 'knock' on the stones and then whisper to them, letting the breath from my voice pass over them. I remind them of their power to ground, steady and defend, and explain to them what it is I need them to do. One way I use anchor stones is to assign them to earth, transform and then reuse any energy directed at the shield to bolster the shield itself. This method takes advantage of energy rather than just repels it. This is great for generalized ill-will.

You can paint (or just trace in holy water or a protective oil) appropriate symbols or sigils for protection on the anchor stones. There are MANY symbols, sigils, and bind-runes that can be used/adapted for this purpose. As always, make sure you completely understand the symbol or sigil you are using.

To use your anchor stones, start them in the center of the protective sphere you visualize. Once the shield is in place and thickened, place the stones around the perimeter of your house or property. If you live in a multi-unit dwelling, place them in each corner inside the bounds of the space that is specifically yours (which may just be one room, if you live in a dorm or share a house with others). Wherever you place one, connect it to the shield in that location.

A shield with anchor stones can last 6 months or more. I refresh my shields every 6 months just to be on the safe side.

This same technique can be sized to a room or subsection of a house. One of the wonderful things about wards is that they're scalable. Simply ward the part of your living space that is 'yours.'

Charms and Folk Practices

There are a host of folk practices and charms for protecting a location, whether that's a house, office or classroom. Some will even work for cars. Here are a few:

Witch bottles: A bottle filled with 'go away' objects – nails, spikes, cat's claws, nettle, urine, etc. It is buried at the edge of your property, tucked into a foundation or wall during construction/renovation, or hidden in the back of a cabinet or behind furniture if you do not have land.

Witch balls: Blown glass balls that generally contain a few strands of glass inside them. The bright colors of the glass attract malicious spirits and energy and the threads trap them.

Evil Eye: Evil Eye charms are generally shaped like a single eye and are blue in color. That particular magickal tech has morphed into a few different forms, including blue bottles or bottles filled with blue beads.

Brooms and Horseshoes: These are deterrents to malicious energy, people and spirits when hung on the wall or above the door of a home. Horseshoes should be hung with the opening facing up. When you move, the broom should be the last thing that comes into the house and it should enter through a window rather than a door. This practice can be pretty entertaining to figure out when you live in an apartment building.

Additional Techniques

Add protective sigils and symbols to the walls of your home. Choose sigils that speak to your personal path. They can be traced in holy water, sacred oils, or energetically. If you are painting a room, paint the sigils on first, then paint the color over top of them, sealing them in. Some sigils are beautiful – they can take the form of knotwork or elegant shapes. If that's the case, feel free to hide them in plain sight. You can include them as part of a wreath or wall hanging, or simply paint them in an appropriate place.

Banishing Pentagram

The Banishing Pentagram comes to us out of Wicca. It is used to immediately send a certain energy away. It can be particularly useful for warding a space temporarily. I routinely use it, followed by Reiki symbols, to guard hotel rooms I'm sleeping in. In a banishing pentagram, the line begins at the lower left hand corner. Visualize something powerful for the line – flames, pure white light, lightning, etc. The phrase I generally use when casting a Banishing Pentagram is "I banish all thoughts, energies and entities that do not serve my highest good."

Figure 10: Banishing Pentagram

One note about banishing: doing too much banishing in our own homes can be detrimental to the spirits that live there. Banishing is a bit like a nuclear blast. Too many blasts, and benevolent spirits tend to seek quieter and less unpredictable residences. Protect yourself, by all means, but use banishing as a last resort.

Going Forward

Magickal Self Defense is an ongoing process with an ever-expanding toolset. You will find specific techniques for shielding and warding that work better for you than others. Remember to experiment here. Shields and wards should all be regularly reset and updated. It can be useful to keep a simple record of when you reset your wards and what the space between resets was like. If you notice that there was either an unusually good or an unusually unlucky period, it can tell you a lot about how well your wards are working.

Close the Ritual of Study as described on page 36.

CHAPTER SIX HOMEWORK

1. Practice the Blackfeather Self-Blessing, Grounding and Centering, and Shielding daily.
2. Continue your short divinatory practice, drawing one or two stones/cards/etc, and looking up the meanings of them. Remember, this is not a divination for the day. It is simply a way to help learn your divinatory tool's language.
3. Continue memorizing the class ritual, opening and closing chants and words.
4. Create and begin working with a semi-permeable or specific permeability shield. Record your experiences with it.
5. If your home is not yet warded, design and implement a shield. Consider what else you would like to incorporate (additional folk practices or sigil magick). Record your shield design and components. Set a calendar notification for three months from implementing your shield to replenish the shield.

CHAPTER 7

THE PRIMAL SPIRIT

For this chapter, you will need this book, your Blackfeather oil, your Blackfeather altar, a device that can play a recording online (if so desired), and your journal.
This chapter includes a lengthy guided meditation, so a comfortable place to sit where you will be relaxed but not in danger of falling asleep can be useful.
Your instructor is Caine and this chapter should take two to three hours to go through.

B egin this chapter by performing the opening of the Ritual of Study on page 20.

THE WAYS OF OLD

One of the most profound unifying behaviors across the entire spectrum of humanity is the practice of healing. Along with the more pragmatic understanding of healing herbs and setting bones, there are thousands of practices based around healing the spirit. Our ancestors understood some ailments are a symptom of soul/spirit damage or loss. This body of knowledge is once again surfacing and proving its value. The powerful healing techniques of Western medicine still have limitations and not everything can be 'fixed' with stitches or an inoculation. Spirit work is an approach to healing that focuses on repairing, restoring, and supporting the soul.

Spirit work is a contemporary practice designed to access healing and visions from the spirit world. This practice is at times influenced or inspired by different indigenous cultures. Like paganism, early spirit workers culturally appropriated some of their practices. As a contemporary path, spirit working seeks to cultivate relationships with the spirit world without using appropriative material. As you grow in your practice, be careful to research the authors and teachers you study with in order to avoid cultural appropriation of closed traditions.

So, what is a spirit worker?

For the sake of clarity, spirit work is not attached to any one specific tribe, nation, or peoples. Healing the soul or spirit, in fact, only loosely belongs to humans. Archeologists have unearthed neanderthal burial sites featuring items and positioning that resonate with the techniques of spirit work. We are building on practices even older than humanity.

The role of a spirit worker is many-fold. In the villages of old, a spirit worker was the therapist, doctor, fortune teller, and emissary of spirit. They were often the strange hermit living just outside of town who everyone was a little unsure of, but who everyone also found themselves needing at some point.

When we think of the healers of old, it's important to understand that a spirit worker's role was ultimately to keep the village alive.

People lived in harsh, dangerous environments that lacked the luxuries we have today. Life was a much more precarious experience when a simple scrape could cause an infection that ultimately resulted in suffering or death. Spirit work is the practice that resulted from trial and error healing. We see practices that fall under the umbrella of spirit work in virtually every civilization on earth.

Sometimes, healing looked like an herbal tea or a poultice. Sometimes, in more dire circumstances, it looked like a spirit worker going into a trance and entreating their spirit guides for intervention or wisdom. Ultimately, the healers of old were scientists without modern day prejudices about what is and is not possible. If they could not understand the problem presented to them, they used whatever means imaginable to gain the necessary knowledge. They were willing to starve themselves, ingest poison, and stay awake for days on the off chance that they might end up in a state of euphoric trance powerful enough to gain some nugget of wisdom to help heal another person, bring life-giving rains, or point the hunters in a direction that would yield a good haul of meat.

At its very core, spirit work is synonymous with healing, whether that is healing of the mind, the body, the soul, or the entire village.

UNIVERSAL TRUTHS

There are some core elements within spirit work that, despite language and distance barriers, exist across the entire planet. I refer to these elements as Universal Truths. Those truths are as follows:

1. Spirit exists, and we can interact with it.
2. Spirits can get sick, and we can heal them.
3. Spirits are smart and can help us.

Working with spirit, and spirits, includes our own souls which we can make contact with, heal, and learn from. Spirit workers use trance to perform something called a "journey." This is the process of leaving our bodies and spiritually traveling to one of several different planes of existence. Accepting that there may be some minor differences in the perception of those planes of existence, they are usually broken down into three general categories.

1. The Upper Realm. This is where divine spirits and ancestors often live.
2. The Middle Realm. The space beside us. The other side of the veil. Try to think of the middle realm as the space between space. It exists all around us at all times, but is just beyond our reach because of the veil. It is where you are most likely to run into spirits of the deceased, fair folk and land spirits, among others.
3. The Lower Realm (or Underworld). This is a place of raw, primordial power. It is where most spirit guides can be found, and where many spirit workers go to seek answers, to seek lost knowledge, and to gather energy to perform tasks. Some divine spirits and ancestors also dwell here.

*Note: Above the above, below the below: Through discussions and personal experience, I have come to understand that there are some external layers beyond the planes of existence listed above. In the underworld, you can find the Fire of Creation. This is raw, universal energy. It is often the stuff we draw upon when we pull energy from below. From above the above, is Divine Golden Light. This golden light is more orderly and also carries powerful healing properties. It is my personal belief that the universe is in balance because of these two forces. The Fires of Creation rise up from beneath and are given direction by the Divine Light. These forces can be interacted with. They can be spoken to. They hold great power and wisdom.

FUNDAMENTALS OF SPIRIT WORK

Compassion. Without compassion, the entire village would have died. Despite the eccentricity of most spirit workers, they must have a deeply rooted sense of compassion. That compassion extends to ALL life since healers hold the whole of nature as sacred. Compassion fuels a spirit worker's willingness to risk their life to do the work they do. Today we have more knowledge of how to safely reach states of ecstatic trance. That helps minimize the dangers on a physical level, but there are still plenty of ways spirit healing can go sideways for the practitioner.

Connectedness. A spirit worker must learn to recognize and respect the interconnectedness of all things. Sickness, especially that of the soul, is often like a puzzle that requires extensive questioning and consideration in order to understand it fully. Spirit workers must be very inquisitive and willing to ask the hard questions in order to dig deep enough to unravel the root cause of an illness.

Creativity. Spirit work is fueled by creativity. The willingness to think outside of the box makes or breaks a spirit healer. Answers might not always make sense at first, but when a trusted spirit teaches us a song and tells us we must smear our faces with ash before we sing it, we paint our faces and sing (with consent, of course). The most powerful tool in a spirit worker's box is their ability to reach a trance state and "hallucinate" on command in order to see and speak with things no one else in the room can see or hear. That requires a level of creativity, and suspension of disbelief, that is not easy to achieve.

Courage. There are many different forms of energy healing in this world and spirit work is the grandparent of them all. It is the primordial soup from which spirituality as a whole was born. It was the early spirit healers who made first contact with Spirit as a means for survival. It takes courage to be willing to face the darkness that can plague the souls of others. Spirit work is a trip into that darkness. It's stepping out of your body, coming face to face with the demons lurking inside another person, and finding a way to pull those demons out and destroy them. All of this, while knowing that you could be poisoned by what you touch.

THE PRIMAL SPIRIT

No two spirit workers will ever be exactly alike. We all have our own spirit allies who teach us different ways to achieve the same ends. I refer to myself as a primal spirit worker, largely because the way I do the work I do involves a lot of animal spirits and a practice called shape-shifting. I have some very strong opinions about being connected to nature and to what I refer to as our primal spirit.

We, as a species, are suffering from the profound disconnect that exists between us and the natural world. My philosophy of primal spirit work is about empowerment through the deepening of that connection. Every aspect of our lives can be further enhanced by making a conscious effort to bring in MORE primal energy.

When we go out into the wild and capture a lion, then put it in a zoo, we know without a doubt that we are still looking at a wild animal. When hundreds of pounds of apex predator look at you, even through the bars of its enclosure, you know down to your bones what you are dealing with. This is because the lion hasn't forgotten what it is.

For thousands and thousands of years humans have slowly drawn an imaginary line in the sand that separates us from that lion, and the rest of nature. As time and technology advanced, we went from huddling in mudhuts to resting peacefully within our very own "people zoos" called cities. Generation after generation of humans slowly allowed themselves to become acclimated to that life. We became domesticated.

We traded our loin cloths and animal furs for jeans and sneakers. We gave up our spears, bows, and clubs in favor of smartphones and e-readers. Thanks to online shopping, hunting and gathering can be done from the luxury of our own bed as we fill our "cart" with pictures of food that will arrive in two days.

But for all of this, we are restless. You can see it when you go to a park and watch how people "oooo" and "ahhh" over a big tree, or a pretty flower. You can feel it in the anticipation you develop waiting to go on a big camping trip, knowing you'll be "away from it all" for a while. There's a reason you enjoy getting away from it all. That reason is your Primal Soul.

The Primal Soul is within all living animals. It is the thing you are seeing reflected in that lion's eyes as it lazily stares a hole through you from its enclosure, knowing it could break you in half effortlessly. It's the reason we get goosebumps when we hear wolves howl. It is why we feel the tug in our hearts at pictures of beautiful landscapes.

That Primal soul wants to be free. It wants to be barefoot in the grass. It wants to be naked under the moonlight. It wants to be raw, passionate, and unchained from the notion that doing so is less than human. Every time we connect with that ancient piece of who we are, we are truly becoming *more* human. The real truth is that humans *are* wild.

Lion...Wolf...Bear...Hawk...*Human*. We share the same energy. We share the same souls. And this practice is going to teach you to reclaim your humanity. You will reclaim your Primal Soul.

Encountering the Primal Self Meditation

A recording of this meditation can be found at blackfeathermystery. com/recordings. It is recommended that you perform this meditation outdoors if possible.

Settle into a comfortable position and let your eyes gently close.

Breathe deeply.

Draw your awareness to your surroundings. Birds chirping, wind blowing. Whatever there may be. Just notice what you notice, and let yourself become fascinated by the world around you.

Allow your attention to center itself on one of those things you notice. Let it consume your awareness for a moment.... Breathe... On the next exhale, allow your breath to blow it away, dissolving the outside world.

Now move your awareness closer. Sense into gravity, and how it gently roots you into place. Allow your entire body to feel cradled by the gravity of Mother Earth.

Breathe....

Gently shift your focus to your eyes. Feel them begin to soften, slowly releasing tension there. Let that release cascade downward, from your eyes...to your cheeks...to your jaw softening. Allow that feeling of relaxation to continue flowing down the back of your neck, out across your shoulder blades....down your upper arms...your forearms. Let your fingers let go of the tension there.

Breathe...

On your next exhalation, feel a warmth in your stomach...spreading outward to soften your core, and chest. Allow that warmth to wash

112

down over your thighs and calves...all the way to your feet and toes. Bask in that warmth.

Sense your heartbeat. Feel it thumping there, beating out the rhythm of your life. Imagine it circulating your blood throughout your body. Allow yourself to take in the sensation of aliveness. This is you. This is your flesh, your blood, your existence. Breathe into that existence. Savor it a moment. Allow yourself to relax in this savoring. To find warm comfort in it as you settle into yourself.

Breathe...

Breathe in....and as you breathe out, let your lungs empty completely. On your next breath, turn your attention inward, beyond the body and into the mind. Here within your consciousness is a vast brightness...a network of interconnected thoughts and ideas weave all throughout this bright space as a soft, luminescent web. In the distance, toward the bottom of the web, you notice an opening.

As you approach the opening, you see a staircase within it.

This is the sacred staircase of your spine, and you will use it to travel downward, step by step, until you reach a gateway located in the center of your heart. Begin to travel down the stairs until you reach the gate.

Only you know how this gate opens...whether by key... by word... or simply by turning a handle.

Open it now and find yourself standing before the garden of your soul. Take a moment to orient yourself...this could be the first time you have ever seen it... or perhaps you come here often. Either way, allow all of your senses to absorb this moment as you step out into your garden.

Feel the earth beneath your feet...smell the richness of the flora here... taste the sweetness of the fresh air that wafts past your face as you step forward.

Listen carefully to the sounds of your garden. Are there birds singing? Perhaps within your garden you can hear music floating softly throughout.

Be at home here... allow the peace of being here wash over you as you take in all of its sights.

There...not too far from you, you see smoke rising. Move toward it.

Winding, twisting your way through your garden, you begin to hear a drum beat. Notice that the drum beats in time to your own heart.

Taking one last step, you come to a small clearing...in the middle of it, you see a campfire. Notice the color of the flames. Watch as they dance and pulse to the rhythm of your heart.

This is the eternal flame of your soul. This is the fire of your life. This is you.

Stand before the fire a moment and watch...listen...

Now, watch as the flames part before you. A figure appears within the fire, becoming more and more distinct. You recognize your long-lost wild side. Your primal spirit.

Notice how it looks at you, how it moves as it steps through the flames and approaches you.

Spend some time here. Take this opportunity to connect with your primal spirit self. Play, dance, or seek wisdom.

The time has come to return and your primal self takes you by the hand, guiding you to the fire.

Watch as the fire grows upward...reaching higher and higher up into the sky. Observe the fire as it becomes a pillar of brilliant gold light.

Before you leave, I want you to look deep into the eyes of your primal spirit self. Ask the question, "What can I do to honor you?"

Once you have your answer, step into that golden pillar of light and allow yourself to rise with it, floating upward above your garden...to gently return to your own body...to right here...to right now.

Breathe....

Take all the time you need. Wiggle your fingers...move your toes. When you're ready, you may open your eyes and begin journaling.

Record your experiences in the Garden with your Primal Self.

MEDITATION, JOURNEYWORK, AND STRENGTHENING YOUR MIND

You will notice an addition to your daily practice in your homework for this chapter: five minutes of meditation. The most powerful, effective way to strengthen yourself magickally, emotionally, and mentally is meditation. Many people approach meditation from a perspective of 'I can't,' thinking they must come to a 'quiet mind' state right away. Nothing can be further from the truth. You see, meditation is power-lifting for your mind. It trains focus and the ability to respond rather than react to both internal and external stimuli. If you get distracted and *notice* that distraction, then return to the focus of meditation, congratulations – you performed a bicep curl for your brain. This returning to the point of focus is the part that strengthens you. Over time, your 'curls' get stronger and more fluid, your focus increases, your discernment improves, and your emotional health becomes more stable.

There are many forms of meditation and it's good to try a few different ones as you begin your meditation practice.

Guided Meditation

Guided Meditation can be useful for people who are just learning to train their brains to focus. They give the listener a script to follow along with, reducing the amount of internal distraction that comes up. At the time of this writing, there are some wonderful free and paid meditation apps. Insight Meditation Timer app includes many free guided meditations. There are also guided meditations of various lengths available on YouTube.com.

To begin using Guided Meditation apps, choose a stress-reducing or mindfulness-based guided meditation. You may need to try a few different guided meditations to find one that's a good fit for you.

Mindfulness Meditation

Mindfulness Meditation comes to us from Buddhism and is very popular in Western culture. In this form of meditation, self-observation is the focus. As thoughts arise, the practitioner simply notices them without engaging with them. A focus on the physical sensations of breathing can be helpful here, returning focus after each thought to the sensation of air moving into and out of the nostrils, the swelling and receding of the belly, or the rise and fall of the chest. This practice is very useful since it does not require a teacher, meditation track, or any additional inputs.

Focused Meditation

Focused meditation uses one of the five physical senses to support concentration. Some examples include gazing at the smoke rising from burning incense (sight, scent), listening to the sound of a singing bowl or other music (sound), or counting prayer beads (touch). As with Mindfulness Meditation, the goal is to return to the subject of focus anytime the practitioner becomes distracted.

Close the Ritual of Study as described on page 36.

CHAPTER SEVEN HOMEWORK

1. Practice the Blackfeather Self-Blessing, Grounding and Centering, and Shielding daily. Add five minutes of meditation between the Self Blessing and Grounding and Centering.
2. Continue your short divinatory practice, drawing one or two stones/cards/etc, and looking up the meanings of them. Remember, this is not a divination for the day. It is simply a way to help learn your divinatory tool's language.
3. Continue memorizing the class ritual, opening and closing chants and words.
4. Journaling Exercise: Write down your favorite memories of nature. This could be your favorite place to go, animals you connected with, or experiences you had.
5. Journaling Exercise: What pieces of your primal nature are you interested in connecting with again?
6. Journaling Exercise: Where do you see the Fundamentals of spirit work within yourself?

CHAPTER 8

THE LANGUAGE OF SPIRIT

For this chapter, you will need this book, your Blackfeather oil, your Blackfeather altar, a device that can play a recording online (if so desired), and your journal. The exercises in this chapter include some that should be performed outside. If your altar space is not part of a living situation where the outdoors is immediately available to you, simply read through the exercises during your study session, then perform them later in the day or week at an outdoor location. Your instructor is Caine and this chapter should take two to three hours to go through.

B egin this chapter by performing the opening of the Ritual of Study on page 20.

Every day we wake up on this Earth, we are surrounded by a cacophony of communications. From the birds chirping, the dogs barking, the bees buzzing, to the neighbors chatting it up at the mailbox, there is a never-ending hum of information exchange. Some of it, like the neighbor, is more easily discerned. But what happens if they aren't speaking your language? Suddenly, their communication can seem very... foreign. We tend to look at animals the same way. "Oh, she just likes to bark," is a pretty famous line my own mother would use about her shepherd. One of my favorite quotes about animal noises is from the Eddie Murphy "Doctor Dolittle" movie. The doctor just begins to realize he can understand the dog, and he says, "You can talk?" To which the dog replies, "What the hell do you think barking is, an involuntary spasm?" The truth is that a lot can be said in a bark despite a lack of shared language. Understanding the content of a dog's bark is similar to understanding the cries of a human baby – a caregiver can often differentiate between the hungry cry versus the wet diaper cry simply because they've taken the time to learn the language of their baby.

Language is a powerful tool. It can help convey deeply abstract thoughts. It can allow us to have long, whiskey fueled conversations about the meaning of life, magick, or our hopes and fears. It suffers greatly, however, from interpretation. Whether we are talking about labels (pagan, witch, spirit worker, etc) or cultural differences, such as an Australian asking you where to find the loo, language is a system of symbols. The word 'shoe' can bring to mind a stiletto, a sneaker, a loafer, or a sandal. Although we use this common symbol system, nuance can get very complicated.

This class is about getting connected to nature. For many of us, this means trying to communicate with both a different language and culture. It also means that the thing you're talking to might not make any sound at all. It might not even be capable of moving or making facial expressions. Nevertheless, learning to communicate with the Beings around us is vital to rebuilding our relationship with nature.

THE RULES

Ted Andrews, the author of <u>Animal Speak</u> among many other titles, and whom I jokingly call Dad, wrote seven simple rules to have what he referred to as "more magical encounters." They are:

1. *Practice seeing and questioning as a child does. Be fascinated and filled with wonder about everything in nature.*
2. *Be a naturalist first. Magic and spirit flows from this and without the naturalist part, the magical shaman cannot be.*
3. *Take trips regularly into nature, at least once per season. Each season brings its own unique offerings and has its own lessons for us.*
4. *Find one special place for you to sit and observe regularly, a place that you can visit throughout the year.*
5. *Observe and be curious about everything. Notice what is going on around you, making notes or sketches of what you observe*
6. *Be unobtrusive when out in nature. Learn to be silent. Try not to talk. Just observe, contemplate and note activity.*
7. *Make your home environment attractive to wildlife. Hang feeders. Put up birdbaths and fountains. Have a variety of plants.*

Ted Andrews, <u>Nature-Speak: Signs, Omens & Messages in Nature</u>, p. 27

As you can see, Ted Andrews considered nature itself to be magick. The connection to nature is a conduit to magickal experiences and workings. This is similar to how one might go about integrating themselves into another culture. Learn about the culture, observe it, honor it, and find respectful and helpful ways to integrate it into your own life.

These rules are a perfect launchpad from which we can begin exploring and connecting to nature. At the same time, we still need the skills required to actually communicate or even just understand what is being said around us.

A Word About Ego

Ego can be the death of any kind of communication. It affects our ability to let go of our own thoughts and opinions so that we may prioritize understanding over expressing. We often take for granted the fact that we have a lifetime of communication experience with other humans. That knowledge base is not as helpful when it comes to communication with the nonhuman world. We must be wholly focused in order to decipher the body language of a deer in the wild. This requires us to step outside of what *we* are thinking and allow ourselves to be solely interested in what is in the mind of the deer. It takes practice, especially when we are excited by the fact that we are face to face with a wild animal.

Escaping ego can be difficult on even the best of days. To do so requires us to be able to rein in our attention to something beyond the constant chatter in our mind. Before you attempt to listen to nature (or anyone really) take a moment to settle yourself. The following are five basic steps that can be done in many ways, but that all need to be taken in order to help center yourself.

1. Set an intention: Calm and center yourself so you have all your listening and observation skills available to you.
2. Focus: Achieving a state of mindful focus doesn't mean we

stop thinking. It means we give our monkey mind something to play with. If breathing works for you, then breathe. If moving helps, move. The point is to put away the internal dialogue.

3. Release: After a bit of practice, you will feel this step arise on its own. Releasing happens when you've settled yourself enough to stop consciously focusing and just immerse yourself in the moment.

4. Accept: Receive whatever the experience may be. Use your observation skills to take it all in.

5. Withhold judgment: Process your experience as objectively as possible. It is so easy to give in to self doubt and criticism. Enjoy the knowledge and experience you gained and file any missteps away as lessons for next time.

EXERCISE: BARE AWARENESS

I mentioned earlier that we exist in an ocean of communication. Not all communication is obvious. Bare awareness as a skill is a combination of all of our six senses being put to work at the same time. It's not just about seeing or hearing or touching, but also opening ourselves up to knowing. Bare awareness takes practice and needs to be built up like a muscle – it is energetically fatiguing in the beginning.

We are, in essence, fine tuning our internal satellite to be able to receive and decode messages we would otherwise normally miss. It is important for us to be able to train ourselves to experience that here in the Physical Realm because as we move forward into things like journeywork, we will become immersed in the intangible. This skill will allow that transition to go much more smoothly and give you the opportunity to practice processing information from the universe.

An audio recording of this exercise is available at blackfeathermystery.com/recordings.

Locate a tree or plant you would like to work with. This can be indoors or outdoors. Position yourself directly in front of that tree or plant.

Stand or sit comfortably and take a few deep breaths. Feel your feet or seat rooted firmly on the floor.

Draw your awareness to your breath. Notice how the air feels, smells, and tastes as it enters into your body. Try to visualize the oxygen as it passes from your lungs into your blood and transports its life-giving energy throughout your body. Allow yourself to experience feeling your flesh being infused with that oxygen.

Shift your awareness to the air outside of your body. Notice how similar the energetic qualities are between what's inside of you and what's outside of you. The same stuff that is giving you life is currently pressing against your skin from all directions. Experience that for a moment.

Bring your focus now to the palms of your hands. There is air touching you, but what else can you notice? Maybe warmth or coolness. Maybe the vibrations of the Earth. Just be curious about what exists. You may get images, or words, or just a general sense of knowing. Just allow whatever comes to come.

Now, shift your focus and let it extend beyond you. Settle your gaze directly onto the tree or plant before you, and allow that same connection you've had with the air to exist between the two of you. Allow the life force of this beautiful creature to communicate whatever it will, however it may.

Give yourself time to connect with this being.

Allow your breath to deepen and lengthen. Feel gratitude toward the tree or plant you were working with and gently direct your attention back to your own body. Wiggle your fingers, roll your shoulders, and return to a normal breath pattern.

Please record your experiences in your journal.

If you are working with a partner or small group, or have a friend who would be willing to let you open to and observe them, repeat this exercise. You can also try it with animals if you have a pet or a home frequented by the local wildlife.

EXERCISE: MEETING THE GENIUS LOCI

Within magick and spirit work there is a spirit role we have come to define as the Genius Loci, or the God of the Land. This is an important mantle that spirits sometimes take on as protectors and healers of their territory. It could be compared to a human taking on the mantle of Priest, Spirit worker, or Witch. When the universe calls, we answer. Such is the life and role of the God of the Land.

These spirits are strong and capable but not omnipotent. They appreciate helpful humans who are willing to offer a bit of energy, clean up some trash, or just sit and talk for a while. The Bare Awareness exercise is a great way to connect and communicate with that guardian spirit. The following exercise is a communion that allows you to exchange energy with the Genius Loci.

First, sit comfortably outside on the earth. Breathe and settle yourself. Extend your dominant hand, palm down, just a few inches above the ground before you. Focus your awareness into your hand and sense the layer of energy between your skin and the ground. Begin to make small counterclockwise circles with your hand, slowly expanding in size. As you do, visualize a portal being opened until it is about the size of a dinner plate.

Inside this opening is a current of raw, beautifully blue fire. This is the energy of the Genius Loci. Reach in with both hands and scoop up some of that fire. Then, wash your head, face and body with the energy three times. If you so desire, this is a good opportunity to invite the spirit to give you messages, including tasks that you could do to help it.

Next, inhale the fire three times, taking long deep draughts of it and allow yourself to be infused with its energy. Each time you do so, breathe out a little of your own energy back into your hands. Then pour your energy into the opening before scooping more of the blue flame.

Once you have finished, it is time to close the portal you've created. Use your hand to make clockwise circles as you visualize the opening slowly shrinking. At the very center, place your receptive hand on top of your dominant hand and press gently downward until you feel the energy snap back into place.

A video demonstrating this exercise is available at:

blackfeathermystery.com/tools/

PLAYTIME

We've just spent time talking about and learning how to connect and commune with nature. That's a great first step. Spend the rest of this study session outside utilizing the skills we have gone over. Look for different trees, bushes, rocks, animals, and even human partners who would be willing to practice the bare awareness technique with you.

The goal here is to learn to build a relationship with nature. In order to do that, it takes time, patience, and practice, just like any other relationship would. Study the flora and fauna around you. Write down all the observations that you can. Consider making a section of your journal your Green Book, where you keep all of your notes about experiences with the natural world. Let yourself stay curious, just as a dog on a walk would be. Think of how often our beloved canine companions pause to sniff or inspect something new. It is that constant effort to understand their surroundings that allows animals to react instinctively to them, generally far more quickly and accurately than humans do.

Most of all, have fun. This is an opportunity to adventure. For so many people, nature remains a thing they water on their desk or watch on their devices. Nature is meant to be *experienced*. The grass is meant to be rolled in. The flowers are meant to be smelled. The cave should be explored. The creek should be splashed in. This is your home. Enjoy it.

When you have finished your session, close the Ritual of Study as described on page 36.

CHAPTER EIGHT HOMEWORK

1. Practice the Blackfeather Self-Blessing, Grounding and Centering, and Shielding daily. Include five minutes of mediation.

2. Continue your short divinatory practice, drawing one or two stones/cards/etc, and looking up the meanings of them. Remember, this is not a divination for the day. It is simply a way to help learn your divinatory tool's language.

3. Journaling Exercise: Where are some places locally you would like to practice the Bare Awareness exercise? What steps do you need to take in order to visit?

4. Journaling Exercise: What can you do to make your home environment more attractive to wildlife? Or, if you do not live in a place where that is an option, what is a way to help support your local wildlife?

5. Journaling Exercise: Environmental Analysis. Choose two different locations in which to practice the Bare Awareness exercise. They should be different – your home and a park, an office and a section of sidewalk near your home, your home and a family member's home, etc. Note the different things you observe in each location. What makes those spaces different? What makes them similar?

Chapter 9

The Empowered Witch Self

For this chapter, you will need this book, your Blackfeather oil, your Blackfeather altar, a device that can play a recording online (if so desired), your journal, your divination tool of choice, a piece of paper (this will be burned) and pen, and a nonflammable dish of some sort . This chapter includes a lengthy guided meditation, so a comfortable place to sit where you will be relaxed but not in danger of falling asleep can be useful. This chapter also includes a Working, so ensuring your study time is uninterrupted is important. Your instructor is Irene and this chapter should take two to three hours to go through.

B egin this chapter by performing the opening of the Ritual of Study on page 20.

EMPOWERMENT PRACTICES

How long have we, culturally, been divorced from our power? A hundred years? A thousand? Survival within a community dictates abiding by the choices of the leaders of that community. Depending on the values and mores of our culture, those survival techniques often include surrendering our sovereignty, repressing our needs, and falling under the power of the ruling class. For long periods of history, to do otherwise was to court death. Our ancestors chose life as evidenced by our presence here, but sometimes at great cost. Along with our physical traits, like eye and hair color, we inherit some of the trauma and struggles of our ancestors. This generation is the first in many centuries to begin working on reclaiming our power. In the Western world, this generation is the first in written history to be able to claim the title 'witch' with reasonable safety, and do the work of magick in the light of day. This generation is the first to be able to do shadow work for our entire familial lines.

We are fighting an uphill battle when it comes to empowerment. We have centuries of inherited programming around making ourselves smaller. Our inherited programming tells us to fit in, to stay quiet, and to keep our heads down. For our ancestors, it was the only way to survive. Our inherited programming is bolstered by current cultural programming. To this day, our larger culture encourages people to be less than they are, to not make waves, to tone it down. This is especially true for women and those with qualities our culture deems 'femme.'

The work of empowerment is a huge part of magick. When we stand in our power, our spells are strong. People who stand sovereign in their strength make for poor targets. When you know who you are, what you want, and how incredibly valuable your life is, you are not as easy to manipulate. Empowered people tend to have healthier boundaries since they have more self-respect. When we look at defensive and protective magick, empowerment is one of the pillars that makes those forms of magick more effective, as well as acting as a deterrent itself.

Becoming empowered is a lifelong process that involves a lot of slips and surges, steps forward and back, hard lessons and necessary discipline. Due to our heritage of subservience, empowerment takes work.

There's a phrase I learned in yoga that I think about when it comes to empowerment: 'root to rise.' On the mat, this means grounding into our feet or whatever part of our body is touching the earth and then strengthening from the floor up. However, this phrase also applies to empowerment. By grounding into our individuality, our sacred selves, we can then draw on that strength to tap into our sovereignty.

Spiritual Empowerment

Your spiritual practice can be tailored to focus on specific areas in your life where you wish to create change. One of those areas should be cultivating an empowered mindset. In the very first chapter of this book, you were taught a self-blessing specifically designed to begin opening you to your own power. The very first altar we build in this course is to ourselves.

This work of focusing on empowerment using our spiritual practices can be expanded. Remember that you can have more than one altar. Indeed, most witch homes I've visited have quite a few (at the time of this writing, I have five). Some are just a cluster of photographs or natural objects, some are elaborate multi-tiered sacred spaces. One technique to consider using when it comes to enhancing your empowerment is the creation of an empowerment altar, vision board or collage.

If you have not created one of these before, a self-work altar/board/collage is a collection of images, words and objects that focus on one particular goal or idea. To create an empowerment altar or board, spend some time thinking about what your Empowered Witch Self looks like, what they do, and how they walk through the world. Then begin collecting images, phrases and objects that you associate with that vision. By cultivating space in your home dedicated to empowerment, you reinforce the message you are sending yourself. Remember, that which is fed increases.

As you are considering spiritual approaches to empowerment, remember that certain deities are more associated with empowerment than others. If working with the Gods appeals to you, you can choose to start honoring and making offerings to an empowered deity. If deities are not something you resonate with, you can choose instead to work with an empowered ancestor. Many of us have an obstreperous grandparent or great aunt or uncle somewhere along the line.

Lastly, remember to include yourself in your healing work. We are trying to heal generations of trauma as well as all the damage we've taken on in this particular incarnation. A good deal of our own power comes through healing the places we carry wounds. Healing work can include many things – self-care, therapy, shadow work, energy work, and healing spells all fall into that category. Part of why people find witches scary is that we can tap into our own darkness to find strength. We are more whole, and more powerful, when we work with our shadows.

Mental Empowerment

Many of us fight some aspect of how our thoughts behave. Our brains are specifically wired to remember bad things rather than good ones. During our evolution as a species, this was a benefit. It was more important to remember that sometimes when the bushes rustle, there's a saber-toothed tiger behind them, than it was to remember how much fun singing around a fire together was. This survival mechanism, though necessary, means that modern day humans wrestle with depression, anxiety and negative self-talk on a large scale. The science at this point indicates that in order to balance out the discordant or depressive thoughts, we have to have a four to one ratio of harmonious or happy thoughts.

The good news is that our brains are learning organs. Neuroplasticity – the ability of the brain to learn new thought patterns – is a very real area of science. There are a few simple things you can do to begin working on rewiring your brain for more empowered thought patterns.

Managing Self-Talk

Start with observation. Write down the negative self-talk you experience. So, if you tell yourself you're lazy, stupid or hopeless, write down those sentences. Don't worry, you can burn this piece of paper later. Once you've observed your self-talk for a few days and have your list together, write down a counter-affirmation for each of those insults. I have personally wrestled with the 'lazy' one. My counter-affirmation is 'I am productive, focused and working hard. I rest when I need to in order to take care of me.'

Now here's the part that's work. When you catch yourself in a negative self-talk pattern, correct it. Think, or say aloud, the counter-affirmation. Do it as many times as it takes. Eventually, your brain learns the new thought pattern and stops sending the old one.

Affirmations

Along with working on self-talk, the use of affirmations is an effective way to influence how our brains behave. An affirmation is a statement we repeat to ourselves that serves to cause or increase a specific behavior or mindset. Affirmations use positive language 'I am' vs 'I am not,' 'I can' vs 'I can't/won't.' Here are a few examples of affirmations I use:

> I am offering myself grace and kindness at this moment.
> I hold my own heart with love.
> I am calm and centered.
> I have all the time I need to do what I need to.
> I am deepening into the present moment and inspiration is
> all around me.

I generally only use three affirmations at a time. Remember that our thought patterns took time to get where they are – they take time to transform as well.

Apologizing

One other area to examine involves apologizing. Many of us apologize frequently for things that we are not at fault for. We apologize for meeting our physical needs. We apologize for talking to someone in customer service even though it is their job to talk to customers. We apologize for expressing opinions even after we've been asked to share them. This has multiple harmful effects – it encourages the idea that our very existence is something we should be ashamed of and apologetic for. It also cheapens true apologies. If someone says they're sorry all the time, it's hard to tell when they actually mean it. Instead of "I'm sorry," begin substituting "thank you." "Thank you for helping me." "Thank you for waiting for me."

"Thank you for being so patient." This takes practice but it does work.

Physical Empowerment

The last layer of empowerment is physical – how we carry and strengthen our bodies. There are lots of subtle physical cues people give off without realizing it. When ill-intentioned individuals are looking to cause harm, they look for easy marks – people who look like they won't fight or resist. By simply adjusting how you walk and stand, you can change the energy you give off. If it is comfortable for you, stand up wherever you are right now.

Start by slouching – slump your shoulders, lower your chin. Take a moment to notice how this feels in your body. Consider how it looks from the outside. You can even go find a mirror to examine how that stance changes your appearance.

Now, roll your shoulders back and down. Stand up straight and let your chin be parallel to the earth. Notice the difference in terms of how this feels. Again, think about how this looks from the outside. Notice the differences if you are looking at a mirror.

Along with practicing standing and walking in an empowered form, remember to avoid looking at your phone or other devices while walking in unfamiliar surroundings. Predators look for people who are distracted or not paying full attention. Also, most of us slump when we look at our phones. Victims of crime are not at fault for the actions of predators, but we *can* make ourselves less appealing as potential targets.

Sacred Movement Practice

Humans like to compartmentalize things. It's an easy instinct to understand – when we break systems into component parts, it makes those smaller areas easier to explore and integrate. This tendency is as present in magick and metaphysics as it is every-where else. One of the biggest compartmentalization conceits we commonly practice is the separation of the physical body from the energetic body and the spiritual body.

Although we can look at the anatomy and function of these three bodies separately, the three systems are ultimately one. These three bodies occupy the exact same space – they are interlinked and inter-woven with each other inextricably. What effects and impacts one effects and impacts the other.

In yoga there is a saying: "Where the mind goes, the body follows. Where the body goes, the mind follows." It's a great illustration of the connection between systems. When we move, relax, open or strengthen a group of muscles, our minds and emotions take that journey as well. It's not a perfect system – having strong legs won't make you emotionally unassailable. BUT, having strong legs will help you feel steadier within your physical body, which will make you feel steadier emotionally, which will give you steadier spiritual or energetic footing.

It is time to add on to your Blackfeather work by developing a sacred movement practice of some sort. No one form of physical movement will work for everyone. Some of us will love going outside for a brisk walk. Some of us will love turning up the music really loudly and dancing around our kitchens for a while. Some of us will love doing yoga, tai chi, bellydancing, or going to a group fitness class. Some of us will love hopping onto a cardio machine at the gym and listening to a podcast. Your movement practice should support you and work within your abilities to keep you free from injury. The point of sacred movement practice is not to become an athlete – it's to better integrate your spiritual practice.

What makes a movement practice sacred? Intention. When I step onto a yoga mat, I do so with intention – with the goal of making my time moving my physical body an offering to and for my Sacred Self.

Your sacred movement practice is one of the most powerful and fundamentally altering things you can do for yourself. It will strengthen your ability to wield energy through a stronger connection to and understanding of your physical body. Doing something that moves and strengthens your physical body helps empowerment on multiple levels. Exercise increases our brain's ability to learn new neural pathways – it helps with the rewiring we've been talking about. What strengthens one, strengthens the others. As above, so below. As within, so without. Feeling physically strong also gives us confidence and helps us move in more natural, comfortable and empowered ways. Part of where my own empowerment comes from is the knowledge that I am strong, capable, and able to function in an emergency. Knowing how to handle physically adverse situations is both invaluable and confidence boosting.

Over the next two weeks, experiment with a few different movement practices. There are many beginner exercise videos on free streaming services to explore. You can try all sorts of different kinds of movement to discover which one you enjoy. Enjoyment is important here – it's very difficult to maintain a movement practice we hate. If I had no choice but to lift weights in order to practice sacred movement, I would not keep up with my physical Work at all. I personally do yoga because I love it for its own sake. I would do yoga even if I didn't need to. Find something that has a similar level of appeal to you.

Three times a week, engage in Sacred Movement practice for a minimum of 10 minutes. If you have friends who are interested in engaging with more physical activities, you might consider joining forces. Find a movement practice you enjoy, and begin to cultivate it.

An empowered mindset includes some mundane underpinnings. One of those practical supports is the confidence in one's capability to function in an emergency. A basic physical self-defense training is a great way to access that knowledge. Many community centers and gyms regularly offer single session basic physical self-defense classes. There are quite a few articles and free video tutorials on simple self-defense movements and techniques available online for free. Moreover, as you explore options for Sacred Movement practice, consider dropping in to a beginner martial arts class.

THE MIRROR JOURNEY

Our adaptive behaviors and shadow impulses are multilayered. Many times, what stands between us and acting from a place of sovereignty and empowerment is the result of lived experience. We all develop different coping mechanisms for dealing with adversity. We are also all subject to social conditioning. Cultivating empowerment includes letting go of structures, ideas, and behaviors that no longer serve us.

When we approach releasing work, it's really tempting to pick the concept or word that comes immediately to mind. The thing is, usually that overall concept – let's say 'self sabotaging behavior' as an example – is the top of a pile of smaller concepts. Our example of self-sabotage could be related to fear, to feeling unworthy, to memories of being abused or picked on, to an external locus of self worth…there are a lot of possibilities. If we try to release the entire concept all at once, we usually find that it was too much. Remember, it took us all quite some time to get to where we are. It takes time and work to undo and regrow the places that have adapted in ways that no longer serve you.

This journeywork piece will take you to the Mirror. Your Mirror is a lens through which to see yourself in many ways. Today, you will be focusing on seeing yourself as the empowered witch you are meant to be.

A recording of the journey below is available at blackfeathermystery.com/recordings.

GUIDED JOURNEY TO THE MIRROR

Close your eyes and allow your breath to deepen and lengthen. Consciously relax your body, starting at the top of your head and working your way down to your neck and shoulders...your chest and back...your lower back and hips...your legs all the way to your toes...your arms all the way to your fingertips.

Draw your awareness to your heart center. Notice a green glow radiating from your heart. This is your life force - raw prana or chi: the magick that animates you and all living things. Become aware of the bright glow of life within you. You might see or sense that energy pulsing in time with your heartbeat.

Your heart center is part of a web of life extending in all directions. Become aware of the lines of energy connecting you to other life. They stretch in all directions – above, below, out to either side.... These pathways hum with creation energy – the raw force of life. Allow some of the energy from the web to flow toward you. Let that green life-energy replenish your heart center, then expand to heal and recharge any areas of your body that need it.

Notice a nexus of that green, fiery energy forming in front of you. It begins to take the shape of a ring of green flame around a center well of darkness. As you watch, the ring begins to expand, moving into a more oblong shape. The dark center takes on a metallic sheen and you realize that a mirror is taking shape before you. Right now, it shows nothing.

When the mirror has finished forming, set an intention to see your empowered witch self. Tell the mirror that is what you wish to see, and touch the surface of the glass. The glass will ripple, and then show you what you have requested.

Look at your reflection. Notice how your witch self stands, how they carry themselves. Notice the differences and the similarities to your-self right now.

Your reflected witch self gestures with both hands and silver ribbons begin to float around the mirror, curling and traveling around the reflection. Each ribbon holds words or ideas that need to be resolved as you travel toward empowered witchcraft.

Reach out to the mirror and pluck a single ribbon. On one side, there's a single word in large print – an overarching concept, behavior, or adaptation that needs to be resolved. Read that word. On the other side of the ribbon will be several words in smaller print – pieces of this overarching concept that can be worked on. Flip the ribbon over to read those smaller words. Choose one word, one smaller piece, to work on. Release the ribbon and watch it dissolve into the air.

Look one last time at your empowered witch reflection. Then, touch the surface of the mirror to clear it, watching it ripple, then become blank once more. The fiery green frame surrounding the mirror will begin to shrink, the prana that formed the mirror dissolving back into the web of life surrounding you.

Begin to deepen and lengthen your breath. Wiggle your fingers and toes, roll your shoulders, gently shift around. Reconnect to your body, to this space, to this time. Take a deep breath in. Let it out on a sigh. Whenever you are ready, gently open your eyes.

Optional Divination

If you returned from your journey with a word to work on, please keep it. If you did not find a word during your journey, get out a divination tool. The question to pose is "What adaptation that no longer serves me is best to resolve right now?" You can work on the next section using the answer your divination tool gives you.

Preparation

Think about your Journey experience and the concept that you want to work on during this session and the next lunar cycle. In your journal, write down:

1. The specific adaptation to be released. Try to get down to one of its smallest component parts if the word you came back with is still a larger concept. Big change requires small steps.
2. A new adaptation to be welcomed. Whenever we release something, we want to be specific about what comes in to take its place. For example, if the small piece you're working on is "fear of my own power," then the new thoughtform you want to invite is "welcoming and honoring my own power."

THE FIRST STEP

Supplies

Along with your Blackfeather Altar (described on page 5), you will need:

- A piece of paper and pen
- A nonflammable dish of some sort
- Your Blackfeather Oil (if it is not already on your altar)
- Your journal
- Your divination tool of choice

On the piece of paper, write the adaptation you are releasing. Remember the specific word(s) for the adaptation you are welcoming (or write it/them down on another piece of paper).

The Working

Stand or sit before your altar. Feel welcome to recast the circle if you would like to (described on page 20).

Light your candle and connect once more to the energy of your Empowered Witch Self.

Read aloud the Highest Self Invocation:

I call my spirit to this place
My highest self, divine in grace
My source of power and direction
Holy is my own reflection
I call my spirit loud and clear
I reach across to draw you here
Standing strong, divine made matter
Aid me as my chains I shatter
Hail, and Welcome!

When you are ready, imbue the piece of paper with the adaptation you are releasing with every bit of emotion and energy around that issue you can access. Carefully light the piece of paper on fire and drop it into the bowl. Watch it burn and feel that particular adaptation receding from your life. If the paper is resistant, feel free to relight it.

Open your Blackfeather oil and put some on the index finger of the hand you write with. Write the word(s) for the adaptation you are welcoming onto your arm. Close your eyes and strongly visualize that new behavior/attitude/belief and what it will do for your life. Imagine how it will change you, and what that change will look like in every way. Once that vision is clear, imagine the visualization moving into your lungs. Take a deep breath and blow the visualization across the word written in Blackfeather oil on your arm.

Hold your hands out in front of you, and close your eyes. Visualize your hands filling with brilliant, clear light. Completely new, completely fresh – benevolent life energy. Divine energy. Allow your hands to fill so much that you can barely make them out through the glow.

Starting at the top of your head, wash away the accumulated shadow, dust and energetic grime you've accumulated. Gently pass that light over every part of your body, cleaning it as you go. Revealing the true colors and forms underneath. If you find that the light starts to dim, simply cup your hands in front of you again and allow them to refill, then continue.

When you have finished clearing the outside of your energy body, draw one hand to your heart and one to your belly, and begin to let that light fill the inside of your body.

When you are completely full and finished purifying yourself, allow your hands to rest comfortably by your sides or in your lap. Take a moment to just sit with your new energy.

Reflection

Please get out your divination tool of choice. Divination is a wonderful way to confirm an effective ritual. The questions to pose to your Divination tool are:

1. How did this Working support my practice?
2. How best can I continue this Work during this lunar cycle?

Write down your experiences with the Working as well as the answers to the Reflection questions.

Ground and center, then close the Ritual of Study as described on page 36.

CHAPTER NINE HOMEWORK

1. Practice the Blackfeather Self-Blessing, Grounding and Centering, and Shielding daily. Include five minutes of meditation, adding in an Elemental focus if so desired.

2. Continue your short divinatory practice, drawing one or two stones/cards/etc, and looking up the meanings of them. Remember, this is not a divination for the day. It is simply a way to help learn your divinatory tool's language.

3. Begin to explore Sacred Movement Practice. If you find a movement style that you enjoy, try to engage in it for a minimum of 10 minutes three times each week. Feel free to experiment and try different movement forms.

4. Journaling Exercise: Write down what being empowered would mean for you. Describe your Empowered Witch Self. Include how they move through the world, what boundaries they set with others, and what practices they follow to support their empowerment.

5. Consider one technique or empowerment support practice from this chapter to add to your practice. Begin to implement that technique.

CHAPTER 10

ELEMENTAL LIFE SCULPTING

For this chapter, you will need this book, your Blackfeather oil, your Blackfeather altar, a device that can play a recording online (if so desired), your journal, and a partner if you are working with one. The exercise in this chapter can also be performed solitary. This chapter is lecture-based with one exercise. Your instructor is Irene and this chapter should take two to three hours to go through.

B
egin this chapter by performing the opening of the Ritual of Study on page 20.

DEATH AND REBIRTH

During the course of a life, it's not uncommon to go through death and rebirth cycles. This occurs anytime there's a big change in our lives, whether we've invited that change (like having a baby) or had that change invade our lives (like a death or breakup).

For my part, in my mid-thirties, I woke up into a nightmare. The life I had built myself was completely out of step with my own values. It did not reflect my ethics or the kind of world I want to build. My immediate circle was peopled with some individuals whose company I would never seek out on my own. I knew that something had to change. I knew that moving so far out of alignment with my true north was destroying me.

I had adapted to trauma. In my case, it was a toxic marriage. But unhealthy patterns can come from many places. Some of us have abusive childhoods or suffer terrible losses. We have histories that include deep shadows and dark waters. We go through a lot as humans, and our psyches do the very best they can with what we survive.

When I decided to destroy the life that was destroying me, I focused strongly on coming back to my own true alignment.

ALIGNMENT

Your true alignment is your personal True North – the form and direction your life naturally follows without the influence of trauma and adaptations to trauma. Even beneath a heavy layer of challenges, defeats, physical and emotional harm, or overburdened lifestyle, your alignment is still there, deep down. That inner voice still speaks. Just very soft at times.

The first time I heard the phrase Divine Discontent, it was from author and teacher Orion Foxwood. Divine Discontent is a restlessness – a feeling that on some level, something isn't right. Frequently, we can't even name what the problem is. For my part, I was married to a systemic abuser, which means my defense mechanisms and ability to perceive harm and abusive behaviors had been eroded over many years. Being a victim of that style of abuse means that you do not realize you are being abused, even when someone is screaming at you or smashing things. However, on a deep level, below conscious thought, I knew something was wrong. If I let my mind get still enough, the restlessness would set in. The need to create, change, or move would become almost overwhelming.

TRIGGERS TO TRANSFORMATION

There are two kinds of realigning or Life Sculpting: self-initiated and invasive. Self-initiated is slightly easier but can be lonely. Many times, in order to realign ourselves, we must choose to sever certain relationships. There's a little meme that goes around periodically that says 'Your vibe attracts your tribe.' Your vibe can also repel the people who are not right for you, especially when you realign. When I reset my life, I lost a lot of friends. It was worth it and removed people from my circle who were unhealthy for me, or unsuited to being companions when it comes to my true alignment. But it did make things a little lonely at times.

Self-initiated Life Sculpting also places you in the position of being the acting agent, which can be more empowered. You are more in control of how your sculpting manifests and what it includes.

Invasive Life Sculpting is more challenging: it occurs when a sudden catastrophe appears in your life with no warning. This can be the abrupt death of someone close, the loss of a job, or a breakup you didn't see coming. There's an additional burden of shock, as well as less time to prepare. During Invasive Life Sculpting, you find yourself starting in the middle of the transformation.

THE ART OF ELEMENTAL LIFE SCULPTING

Most of us live in a constant state of stimulus-response. We are reacting to our world rather than initiating change. Life Sculpting puts the driver's wheel back into our hands. It's an intentional, deliberate way to change or redirect a life path. Many times, we wish for change but don't actually sit down to examine how to address that desire and then make a plan to manifest it. The first thing to do is sit and explore what our natural alignment actually is.

This exploration involves firm, focused introspection and visualization. There's a lot of journaling involved. Give yourself time for this – it can take weeks or months. Dream big and get it *all* down before moving forward. We align ourselves by figuring out how we orient to and connect with the five primal Elements of Earth, Air, Fire, Water and Spirit.

Earth

Earth is where we send our roots, and is the way we manifest how and where we want to live. The first question to sit with is 'What lifestyle fits you best?' If you were starting with a blank slate right now, how would you choose to live? For example, my former spouse preferred a consumptive lifestyle. There was an almost constant parade of boxes arriving at the house due to their purchases. Although I could live in that environment, my Earth alignment is more minimalistic. I purchase things I need, or objects that truly bring me joy and beauty, but I keep a pretty low quantity of stuff overall.

What are your priorities? How important is fiscal security to you? Are you comfortable winging it, or do you need a steady, dependable paycheck of a certain amount? What do you actually *need* in order to live? Our culture constantly pushes the idea that more is better, but it's simply not true. There is a state of 'enough' for each person. Figure out what yours is.

Once you have identified, visualized and journaled about those first two areas of inquiry, you can peel back the next layer: What does your ideal lifestyle look like? Does it include an apartment? A house? Roommates? Do you have a yard? A few acres? An entire farm?

The next layer is aesthetic. What does your ideal home look like? Is it warm and cozy, full of books, cats and knicknacks? Is it open and airy? Is it clean or cluttered? Calm or stimulating? What colors are present? What colors, textures and artistic styles make you feel safe? This is different for everyone. You have an alignment here – write down what it is.

If you really have no idea what your own taste is due to indulging the preferences of others, start a Pinterest board for this. Begin looking at house and room designs and save the ones you like. Over time, you'll begin to see what your aesthetic is based on what you think is beautiful.

Air

Air is how our mind is served by our lives. It's our thought patterns. It's our work, our mental state, and our play. Start by examining work. Rather than being specific about what exactly you do, or will do, place more importance on how it will feel and impact you. What kind of work is good for your mind? Are you extroverted or introverted? What skills do you enjoy using? People have different innate abilities – organization, creativity, communication, steadiness. What are yours?

How do you want your thought patterns to behave? Consider your current common mental states. You can even use a tracker here for mood. There are some good apps that help identify regular mindsets. Once you've noticed your thought patterns, consider what you would change. How would you adjust your self-talk? How do you want to nurture your mind? Will you have a meditation practice? A movement practice?

Play gets short shrift in this culture, but it's absolutely vital for health across the board. Engaging in play stimulates creativity, reduces stress, increases our sense of well-being, and depending on the kind of play, we sometimes experience physical gains in strength and flexibility. Play also helps us connect to our inner child – one of the deepest layers of identity. For many people, childhood was fraught with difficulty. Allowing our inner child to have healthy moments of play is a powerful way to heal some of our oldest psychospiritual wounds.

So, how do you want to play? What hobbies interest you? What do you always wish you had more time for?

Fire

The realm of Fire governs our passions as well as how we burn – how we spend – our time. Some of this will be harder to identify. When we are spending energy and emotion maintaining a misaligned lifestyle, we don't realize how many reserves we have. That said, these questions are still worth considering:

How do you want to experience passionate love? With a partner? With an activity? With a community? What does passionate love look like for you? Is it romantic or platonic? If you are romantic, are you monogamous or polyamorous? Prepare to be honest going forward with your partners, communities and friends. Be specific and verbal about your wants and needs. No one can intuit all your needs all the time.

What boundaries do you want to set when it comes to time? Time equals both money and energy, and there is a dollar value to happiness. There's a dollar value to rest and recovery. Before I ended my marriage, I was a workaholic. I think some of that was an attempt to escape from my spouse, but some of it is due to a tendency toward obsessive behavior. I have very firm boundaries now around the hours I work. I'm a contractor, which means the more I work, the more money I make. However, I place more value on my relationship with my spouse, and on my ability to rest and recover, than I do on financial gain. Everyone needs to figure out their own balance here, and what boundaries to set in order to support that balance.

Water

In this prism of looking at our lives, water is our bodies. Our brains and hearts are composed of 73% water. Our lungs are about 83% water. Our skin contains 64% water, muscles and kidneys are 79%, and even our bones are watery: 31%.

Start by letting go of how you want to look in the fantasy universe. Some aspects of appearance are not negotiable. They also trigger all sorts of society-fed bullshit. Consider instead: How do you want your body to feel? More rested? More flexible? Stronger? Better fed or hydrated?

What physical activities do you want to be able to do? Hiking, dancing, making pottery, and playing guitar are all physical activities that require certain kinds of movement. What movements do you want your body to be able to make?

Spirit

The realm of Spirit governs our connections: to the Divine, to other humans, to the self, to the sacred earth.

In your aligned life, what does your connection to Spirit look like? What kind of relationship is it? What does it include? Would you like to add more prayer and meditation? More ritual? More dedicated shrine/sacred space within the home? Outdoor shrines?

How do your connections to other humans support you? What qualities do your friendships include? Try not to think of specific individuals, but of the nature of the connections you desire. What are some traits of those friendships and people? What are the outlooks of your desired friends? How do they treat others and themselves? Remember that one person can't be expected to fulfill all your physical, psychological, and emotional needs all the time. A group of trusted people is needed, and often a therapist! People who are raised male in the United States in particular are trained to believe that their romantic partner should fulfill all their needs, all the time. That belief is toxic, dangerous, and sets everyone in the relationship up for suffering. So, think about what healthy, balanced friendships look like for you.

As an example, before I left my marriage, I had a wide social circle. I was known for throwing large parties at which any number of crazy things could happen. However, most of those friendships were very shallow. Many of the people in my sphere at that time were self-destructive, mean or gossipy, apathetic, or social climbers. What's interesting now, years later, is that my social circle is roughly the same size. However, it's made up of deep bonds with people who are really walking their talk when it comes to creating beauty and connection in the world. My social circle inspires me.

How will you stay connected to your Sacred Self? How will you support your true alignment? How will you keep yourself accountable to you? What systems can you put in place to better hear your True North speaking? How will you care for yourself? What can you do to better support your own journey?

YOUR FIRST SCULPT

Once you've dreamed, introspected and written out your vision for your true alignment, you may feel overwhelmed with how to begin. That's part of why I break sculpting into the Elements. Return to your journal and for each Element write out a few simple, small steps you can take to begin bringing your life into alignment there.

For example, if your ideal home (from the Earth section) is open and airy and you live in a cluttered environment, you could write down "Spend 10 minutes per day/30 minutes once a week (whatever fits your schedule) purging your belongings." If you feel like your Air alignment would be better served in a different line of work, update your resume. Choose some small boundaries to start with for Fire – set a specific time each week when you will not be available online or via phone. If your Water alignment would be served by getting more rest, start going to bed a little earlier. Even if it's just 10 minutes. Or, prepare for the next day in the evening so you can sleep in a little later in the morning. Support your Spirit alignment by creating a little more space for the sacred in your life. Or, begin to purge your connections on social media. Foster the friendships whose qualities match your alignment. Begin to draw back from the ones that do not.

Then, from that list of small steps, pick one. Maybe two. Start with those. As those changes begin to take hold and draw you closer into natural alignment, you can add on. And if something happens where a massive life reordering is going to occur, you now have a full blueprint for a rebuild.

SOME PRACTICES TO CONSIDER IMPLEMENTING

A Book of Paths

A Book of Paths is a binder or journal for your integrated, aligned life. Include the visioning for each element, your intentions going forward, track your affirmations, and enter spells and rituals that support your alignment.

Dark Moon Check-Ins

I'm a huge fan of this tool and it has proven very useful for me. At each Dark Moon, check in with yourself, your partner or family as necessary. Are you on track? Do you have anything you need to air out or talk through? What are working on for the next lunar cycle? What is your intention or affirmation for that time? Check-ins are specifically used for helping yourself and your closest loved ones – it's not for airing grievances but for finding solutions. A useful conversation prompt is 'What do you need this month, and how can I support you?'

JOURNALING EXERCISE

The following question and answer exercise can be done with a partner or as a journaling exercise.

If you are working with a partner, one of you will be the Questioner and one will be the Responder. After each question, the Questioner will say 'Thank you' and then ask the next question. No other words are necessary here – this is an opportunity to practice listening and supporting another person's process. The responder can repeat answers or simply say 'I don't know' if they run out of words.

If you are using your journal, you will simply act as the Responder.

The two questions are:

Where do you feel most aligned in your life?
Where do you feel most misaligned in your life?

To perform this exercise, answer (or ask/answer with a partner) each set of questions three times. Remember that you can say or write 'I don't know' if you run out of words by the third round of questions.

When you have finished your session, close the Ritual of Study as described on page 36.

CHAPTER TEN HOMEWORK

1. Practice the Blackfeather Self-Blessing, Grounding and Centering, and Shielding daily. Include five minutes of meditation, adding in an Elemental focus if so desired.
2. Continue your short divinatory practice, drawing one or two stones/cards/etc, and looking up the meanings of them. Remember, this is not a divination for the day. It is simply a way to help learn your divinatory tool's language.
3. Continue to explore Sacred Movement Practice. If you have a movement style that you enjoy, try to engage in it for a minimum of 10 minutes three times each week.
4. Journaling Exercise: Begin your reflection, visioning and journaling process for the Earth section of Elemental Life Sculpting. Your entry should include answers to all of the questions in the Earth section of this class.

CHAPTER 11

BEGINNING JOURNEYWORK

For this chapter, you will need this book, your Blackfeather oil, your Blackfeather altar, a device that can play a recording online (if so desired), and your journal. This chapter includes some journeywork, so a comfortable place to sit where you will be relaxed but not in danger of falling asleep can be useful. Your instructor is Caine and this chapter should take two to three hours to go through.

B egin this chapter by performing the opening of the Ritual of Study on page 20.

Take a look around you. All around you is "stuff." Even the human bodies we inhabit right now are just a complex configuration of basic elements that you can find in any high school chemistry lab. What you are seeing is only a part of a much larger whole, a much bigger picture that includes existential truths to which our five mundane senses just cannot connect. Reality is not purely created of physical, tangible **stuff**. It's deeper than that and, much like onions and ogres, it exists in layers. So many of us go our entire lives living in a half-lie, missing out on the hidden truths of our existence. In this lesson, we are going to take a look behind the curtain. You will get to glimpse into a part of reality not often seen. Understand, though, that this isn't even the tip of the iceberg. Wonderland is only the first stop down the rabbit hole. The skills we will be going over are meant to let you open the door so that you may begin what I hope will become one of the most rewarding journeys of your spiritual practice.

STATES OF CONSCIOUSNESS

The first thing to understand about journeying is that it requires us to shift out of an ordinary state of consciousness. One of my favorite sayings is "it is the spirit worker's job to hallucinate on command in order to see that which others cannot." There are a lot of different ways that we can get ourselves into that particular state of consciousness. In the past, many of those methods involved ingesting potentially dangerous combinations of herbs, roots, and fungi in order to force our brains to let go of ordinary consciousness. It worked great, but carried an unnecessary cost that we no longer have to pay. Thanks to science, we have a deeper understanding of how our brains work and how to manipulate them safely into producing the same state of altered awareness that once took rolling the dice with our health to achieve.

Meditation and altered consciousness require a specific pattern in our brains. In our normal state of consciousness, we exist in what is referred to as the **beta** wave state. Here, our brains are humming along at approximately 14 to 30 cycles per second. In the beta state, we are active, alert, and interacting with the world around us. This means anything from reading a chapter about spirit work to laying on your car horn in rush hour traffic. In the beta state, we are much less likely to be aware of subtle energies. We are essentially distracted by our own brain activity and solidly existing within the physical realm.

The next stage of brain activity is referred to as the **alpha** state. Alpha is a bit slower (9 to 13 cycles per second or cps), and is what I would refer to as relaxed awareness. In this state, we are lucid and aware but not actively using our brain. We are, in essence, a car at a stop light. The engine is running, but not forcing anything to happen. Often we get here when we take a moment to relax. Sitting out in nature, laying in the bathtub with a glass of wine and some chocolate, and quietly waiting in line at the grocery store are all good examples of alpha. On the lowest end, closer to 9cps, is where we often experience those moments of being "spaced out." It's where you sit on autopilot long enough that your brain stops recording and just kind of skips over the past few seconds or minutes. Around this frequency is also where people tend to begin to see the edges where the physical and metaphysical realities overlap. Things move in the corners of our vision. Soft sounds that aren't quite there may catch our attention and be gone in an instant because it was just enough to nudge our brain waves back upward into a more alert state of consciousness.

Then, we have the **theta** wave state. At somewhere between 3 to 9 cps, our very perception of reality can make a huge shift. Those things living just out of focus can suddenly be looked at directly in the eyes...or some approximation of eyes. This is the liminal space between being awake and asleep. It is where we find ourselves when we are drifting off and suddenly feel as if we are falling. The theta state is the journeywork state of consciousness. Here we are not only aware of the other realms but able to traverse their endless landscapes, beginning a process of discovery and empowerment that will easily last the rest of this lifetime.

It is important to understand that the things you see and do while journeying are very, very real. It is through journeying that I do my work as a healer. By stepping from ordinary consciousness, I am able to do things in other worlds that affect people right here in this one. Proficiency takes training and practice, but the fact remains that what you experience during a journey can and will follow you back to ordinary reality. Much like being in the real world, there are both great rewards and potentially terrible consequences. The trick to avoiding bad things happening while journeying is exactly the same as it is here in the material realm. **MAKE GOOD CHOICES.** If we drive while drunk, we could crash. If we get in a stranger's car we could end up in a dusty basement putting lotion on our skin. Smoking can cause cancer. Too much chocolate is why I'll never be skinny. If a spirit you know nothing about asks for you to offer it your blood so it can teach you "secrets," it's a good opportunity to practice boundary setting. If you walk into a dark alley and find a glass bottle of glowing liquid, you wouldn't drink it without at least sniffing it first. The same applies in the other realms. Ask questions, even if they seem obvious. Don't sign a single contract without reading the fine print, and you'll do just fine.

THE UP, THE DOWN, AND THE IN-BETWEEN

There is no known limit to the places that one might see while journeying. However, there is a general understanding of three basic realms of existence. I tend to look at them more like directions toward which one can travel. Although the inner workings of journeying are a little more complicated than this we can basically go up, down, and side to side. Those correspondences come with three generally accepted titles.

Going down means going to the underworld, or lower realm. The underworld is rife with raw magical energies, spirits, and lost knowledge. It is here where spirit workers meet a majority of their helpers and do most of their self work. It is important to understand that we always begin our path as a healer by healing ourselves. Self understanding and empowerment is vital to being able to help others. The underworld contains most of what we will need in order to do that work. You can also find some deities and ancestor spirits in this realm. The further down you go, the less tangible things will seem. As I mentioned before, everything is in layers. The first stop is generally something that looks like a natural landscape. Beneath that, you're likely to find something akin to caves and tunnels, or vastly deep bodies of water. As you travel further down, you may run into areas of pure energy. It can feel a bit like swimming through static. Under the underworld exists the wellspring of raw creation. This powerful Source is sentient, and it is what we draw upward when we pull energy from "below." I would not call traveling to it a beginner's project. You want to wait until you feel comfortable journeying in places that seem familiar. A forest can seem familiar even if we run into the Cheshire cat. A purely discorporeal plane of existence within which time, space, and **you** have no real definition, not so much.

Going up means traveling to the upper world, also called the ascended plane. This is a place where you are most likely to run into beings of light, deities, and ancestors. It is possible to find helpers and guardians here, but not nearly as likely as the underworld. As a spirit worker, most of my time spent in the upper world is limited to having conversations on behalf of other people. There are always exceptions to rules when it comes to spirit, though, and I have a 'workstation' in the upper realm where I perform some of the work I do. If the lower realm contains knowledge, the upper realm contains wisdom. The lower realm is raw, the upper realm is organized and refined. Neither is better than the other. Both certainly have their place, even if you prefer to work more with one kind of energy than the other. It is definitely valuable to recognize the importance of each. Again, the further you travel, the less familiar things will become. It is definitely possible to travel upward to a point where you will find yourself at an infinitely powerful source of sentient energy. I am not one to speak in definitives when it comes to things like spirit. This energy has wonderful healing properties, and it is from here that we draw down light to help ourselves and others be well.

Last, we can move side to side. This is often referred to as the middle realm. It is just on the other side of the Veil – the boundary that separates the visible and tangible from the invisible and nontangible – and home to everything from the fae to lost souls. It is also where parasitic shells and shell fragments float around looking for hosts. The middle realm is an easy place to do direct healing work for other people. Traveling here is a great way to connect to the Genius Loci/ Lord of the Land. When we experience spirits while in the beta or alpha brainwave states, it is usually because they are in the middle realm. Those are the moments that I mentioned earlier where it can seem like you could see that shadow if it would just hold still.

Riding the Horse

I mentioned earlier that we have much better ways to reach the theta wave state than swallowing poison. Thankfully, due to a combination of science and cross-culturalism, we now know that we can use something as simple as a good drum beat to alter our brain waves. Other things such as dance, staring into firelight, and some practices involving chanting or singing can get us there. A lot of it has to do with training and figuring out what works best for you.

In this lesson, we are going to be using drumming to draw your brain waves into a state that will hopefully allow you to experience the journeying state of consciousness. Drumming is a powerfully primal sound, and it tends to do very well at triggering instinctive reactions. The sound of a journey drum is compared to horse's hooves clapping on the ground and so is often referred to as "riding the horse." That association of listening to a herd of horses galloping by can evoke some pretty powerful feelings.

There are some important points to understand before we begin.

First, not everyone experiences journeying the same way. Some people can see, some have a sense for what is happening around them, but no visual cues, some people are only able to hear, some have a fully immersive experience. I know a handful of healers for whom journeying is an internal narration akin to listening to an audiobook. None of these experiences are better or worse than any other. No matter what you receive, it is much more useful to focus on what is there than to allow yourself to get caught up in wondering what you're missing. It is my position that the universe will present itself to you in a way that you can receive. So, if all you get are smells, the chances are good that you're probably already better at interpreting scent than most of the population. Most people experience fragmented versions of our five basic senses. Journeying is also a cumulative exercise: the more you do it, the more strongly you are likely to experience it. If you start off with a lot of fuzzy images during the following exercises, within a few months of prac-tice, you will probably see very clearly. More than anything, try simply to allow yourself to enjoy the wonder of experiencing these other planes of existence. This is the cool part of being a spirit worker. Let yourself have fun.

Next, there are three phases to a journey which are marked by three distinct drum patterns.

The first is the intention setting. It is best to use a slow drumming pattern here that repeats three times and allows for you to set your intention very clearly with each repetition.

The second is the journey and will consist of a steady rhythm somewhere around 200 beats a minute. This can go on for any amount of time. The typical journey lasts between 10 to 30 minutes. For the purpose of this chapter, our journeys are only going to last about 5 minutes at a time.

The third phase is known as the call back. At this point in the journey, the rhythm will shift suddenly and become more erratic. It is meant to stimulate your brain and begin increasing your brain waves so that you come back to an ordinary state of consciousness. This is a time when you should wrap up whatever it is that you're doing during the journey and travel back to your body. Please note that distance does not work the same way in spirit as it does here. Even if you feel as if you have traveled millions of miles from your body, you need only a moment to will yourself back.

Recordings of journey drumming are available at blackfeathermystery.com/recordings. For this exercise, we will be using the five-minute journey drumming track.

FIRST SERIES

This first set of journeys is meant to get you used to the drumming and to allow you the chance to start stretching your spirit legs. Once the actual journey beat begins, it may take you some time to settle into the theta state. This is fine. It's why we're here. We will begin with three very simple journeys. I am going to give you the intention that you will set during the first phase of a journey. Make that intention your primary focus. Do your best to focus only on the intention. There will be parts of you that want to question whether or not you're going to experience anything. There will be a part of you that wants to focus directly on the drumbeat. There may be a part of you that wants to focus on everything that has happened today leading up to this moment. It is okay for those things to happen. Notice when distracting thoughts come up, take a breath, and then refocus on your intention.

For each exercise, settle comfortably into a position where you are supported, but not in danger of falling asleep. Play the recording and close your eyes. Say each intention to yourself **three times** during the intention setting phase of the recording.

Intention #1: I am going to see myself.
(The goal here is to step outside of your body into the
middle realm and turn to look at yourself.)

Intention #2: I am going to travel to the lower realm.
(Now that we're able to get out of ourselves, you will take
the next step of moving downward. If you get to the underworld, have a seat for the rest of the journey. Take note of
what is around you, and do nothing else.)

Intention #3: I am going to find a guide.
(Next, you will go back to the underworld and send out a
call for help. Focus on asking for a guide who will help you
get used to journeying.)

Be sure to record your experiences with the three exercises above in your journal. Remember that you can repeat these journeys as needed.

PLACES OF POWER

The other realms are places of infinite possibility and part of journeying is seeking self-empowerment. Putting those two concepts together, we can begin to work on shaping energy for our own purposes – you have the power within you to create what exists. One of the first actions we want to take when exploring spirit work is to build a seat of power. Consider it your secret superhero hideout. These places are meant to connect you with your own mojo. They are where you can learn more about yourself, about your unique path, and to help answer important questions like "Uh... what do I do next?"

For each exercise, settle comfortably into a position where you are supported, but not in danger of falling asleep. Play the recording and close your eyes. Say each intention to yourself **three times** during the intention setting phase of the recording.

Intention #1: For this journey, your intention will be to find your place of power. We may have many that we find over time. For this moment, you want to focus on the one you need right now. Consider it your starter home. You will travel to the underworld, meet with your journey guide, and then ask to be taken to your place of power. If/once you get there, do nothing.

Intention #2: This time you will travel to your place of power again, then ask to be shown what the purpose of this place is, and how you can best maintain your connection to it.

Intention #3: For your last journey, you will travel to your place of power, sit in it, and ask to be infused with its energy so that you may bring it back to your body.

Be sure to record your experiences with the three exercises above in your journal. Remember that you can repeat these journeys as needed.

Further Practice

Whether you were able to complete the exercises listed above easily or are struggling, you need to practice. The following is a list of intentions for you to use as you develop your journeying skills. You can use any of them in any order. You may only use one repeatedly. Do what you feel lets you progress, even if it's only tiny bits at a time.

I journey to my place of power to continue my work.
(This one alone can be a huge undertaking. Stick with it.)

I journey to my place of power to seek answers to questions.

I seek to work with my journey guide.

I journey to explore the landscape of the underworld.

When you have finished your session, close the Ritual of Study as described on page 36.

CHAPTER ELEVEN HOMEWORK

1. Practice the Blackfeather Self-Blessing, Grounding and Centering, and Shielding daily. Include five minutes of meditation, adding in an Elemental focus if so desired.

2. Continue your short divinatory practice, drawing one or two stones/cards/etc, and looking up the meanings of them. Remember, this is not a divination for the day. It is simply a way to help learn your divinatory tool's language.

3. Continue to explore Sacred Movement Practice. If you have a movement style that you enjoy, try to engage in it for a minimum of 10 minutes three times each week.

4. Journeywork: Choose an intention from the Further Practice section of this chapter and use one of the journey audio tracks located at blackfeathermystery.com/recordings to practice journeying. Aim for three practice sessions per week. Remember to ground and center yourself before and after each journey. You do not need to create and release ritual space unless you would like to.

5. Journaling Exercise: Begin your reflection, visioning and journaling process for the Air section of Elemental Life Sculpting (chapter 10). Your entry should include answers to all the questions in the Air section of this class.

6. Select an intention listed in the Further Practice section of this chapter or repeat the exercises from the First Series and Places of Power sections. Try to practice journeying at least once per week using the material from this chapter.

CHAPTER 12

BEGINNING SPIRIT HEALING

For this chapter, you will need this book, your Blackfeather oil, your Blackfeather altar, a device that can play a recording online (if so desired), your journal, and your partner if you are working with one. All exercises can also be performed solitary. This chapter includes some journeywork, so undisturbed study time is important. Your instructor is Caine and this chapter should take two to three hours to go through.

Begin this chapter by performing the opening of the Ritual of Study on page 20.

NEITHER HERE NOR THERE

Previously, we discussed the idea of journeying as a process of movement. The entire basis of the concept of journeying is that, with effort and proper guidance, we humans are capable of leaving our physical bodies behind and traveling into different realms of existence where we may explore the world of spirit. We use specific visualizations such as looking for a hole to travel downward, or rising with smoke or light to move upward. The entire practice itself is even called "journeying" (in case you forgot).

Now, consider the possibility that the journey itself is a metaphor designed to allow our minds to more readily accept the experience. Humans frequently have delicate sensibilities. The concepts of linear time and space are ones we need to clutch tightly in order to feel comfortable with reality. If you are familiar with computer speak, you have probably heard of the term Graphical User Interface or GUI. The screen of your smartphone is a GUI designed to allow us to execute complex tasks by just touching or dragging things around. It gives us icons and links and an intuitive interface to open and close programs. That makes the whole experience of operating a device user-friendly. The interplay of our five senses can be seen as similar to how a smartphone operates. Our senses allow us to take information from all around us and distill it into a very tangible world with which we can interact. Using sight as an example, we can see because light is reflecting off of things. That light hits our corneas, then is sent to our brain by way of the optic nerve, and then decoded there into a mostly cohesive image so that we can so we can look at our smartphones and watch society unravel in real time. The moment light has been removed from a room our vision fails us. Light is a super high-frequency energy vibration. Our ears pick up vibrations that are much lower frequency and translate that into sound so that we can hear notifications from our phones when a friend contacts us. One important thing that these examples have in common is electrons.

In previous chapters, we explored the idea that reality consists of different layers of energetic existence. Electrons and other subatomic particles are the building blocks of those layers. Even our own auras are composed of these particles. Just as our body is made of elements that can be found in a high school chemistry room, our soul is made of things that also make the rest of the universe. Thanks to some techno wizardry, scientists and engineers devised a way to photograph energetic bodies. In his book, <u>Vibrational Medicine</u>, Dr. Richard Gerber discusses an experiment using a leaf with a hole cut into it. A photograph of the leaf's energetic body showed within the empty space, a perfect image of that exact same leaf. This photograph understandably sparked a lot of discussion. Dr. Gerber explains how this relates to something called the Holographic Principle. The core concept of the Holographic Principle is that every piece contains the information of the whole. DNA is used as a common example to help people wrap their heads around this idea. Every cell within you contains the blueprint required to build an entire YOU.

Going even further down the rabbit hole, the same photographic technique was used on lizard embryos. In doing so, the researchers observed that the energetic signature they were photographing – the energy body – of the embryo took on the form of an adult lizard. The same also applied to saplings of trees, leaving us to deduce the possibility that our energy body behaves similarly when it comes to our DNA. It comes fully formed and with all the information needed to produce the final outcome of our physical body. This means that our spirit body is effectively a holographic energy field.

The reason this is important is that there are theoretical physicists who believe our *entire* universe may be a giant energy interference pattern with the same characteristics. In theory, just as the empty space within the leaf (which was still within the greater whole of both its physical and energetic bodies) contained all the information for rebuilding that leaf, all space around us contains *all* the information of the universe. All it takes is decoding one tiny piece of the hologram to unfold the entire matrix. Because that hologram is made up of energy, humans who train to tap into and receive energy are effectively unlocking the entire universe at once and selectively using only what we need of it.

Here's the thing. That's a truckload of information in a tiny space. Unless you're a yogi or a monk whose entire life is dedicated to ascension, it is unlikely that you'll be able to wrap your head around the entirety of the universe at once. Going back to my opening statements about journeying as a metaphor, we use visualizations and meditation to allow us the opportunity to tap into small portions of that tremendously dense information. Journeying is, essentially, Microsoft Windows: The Universe. It creates a graphical user interface that allows us to only see what we need to see, interact with what we need to interact with, and make huge changes (such as deleting a possession from the registry files of your spirit) manageable through tangible cues similar to when we drag-and-drop something into our computer's recycling bin.

Now that you've had the opportunity to explore journeying a bit, we are going to begin to customize your desktop.

SHORTCUT.EXE

I've had more than one person tell me they worried that they'd done something wrong because they never saw a hole in the ground at the beginning of their journey. Instead, from the moment the drums started, they were walking around in the underworld. This caused them to second guess and internally invalidate their own experiences. Taking everything we've learned about the holographic principle, you can begin to understand why a lot of the journey is a metaphor. Using visualizations of actual travel is a really good way to learn to navigate the universe, especially when you're looking for something/somewhere you've never been. Most people need that in order to at least find their sea legs. This way, when you set your intention to go back to the same place, there is a route already laid out in your subconscious. However, shortcuts are a very real part of journeying. If this happens to you, don't discount it – you may simply have adapted quickly to journeywork.

The method with which you travel matters a lot less than what you do with it. Some of us need to see the landscape passing by to find what we are looking for. Some of us do not. Most importantly, rest assured that you are journeying "right" regardless of whether or not you experience it as movement or as teleportation.

Place of Power Exercise

For this first exercise, please visualize your place of power from the exercises in chapter eleven. Close your eyes, take a few deep breaths, and just recall as much of it as you can. Rebuild your place of power here in your mind, in this space. Give yourself a couple minutes to gather as much detail as you can, then open your eyes and take in your surroundings.

Using the recorded five-minute journey track located at blackfeathermystery.com/recordings or simply using a five-minute timer, do a brief journey. The intention for this journey is to go to your place of power. This time, instead of looking for a tunnel to dive into, think of the process as closing your physical eyes here in this room and then opening your astral eyes within the space of your place of power. Once you get there, spend a little time drawing in some energy to fuel you for the rest of the work we will be doing in this chapter. When you hear the callback in the drumbeat, return to your body and gently open your eyes.

ELEMENTAL HEALING EXERCISE

In previous chapters, we explored sharing energy in a spirit working sense. This channeling of energy through ourselves allows us to pass that energy into another person or being. People trained in Reiki learn how to do the same thing across distances of not only time but space as well. Using journeying, we can eliminate the boundary of physical distance in energy work.

There are two approaches to this exercise depending on whether you are working with a partner or small group, or working independently. Please choose the one that best suits your situation.

Partner/Small Group Exercise

Partner up with one or two people. One person in your group will be the "healer" and the other(s) is going to be the "recipient(s)". These roles will rotate so that your group has the chance to experience both roles. In this exercise, the healer will direct positive, life-giving energy to the recipient. 'Positive' energy can look like many different things, so the recipient should choose which elemental energy serves them best right now: earth, air, fire, water, or spirit. The healer will channel that elemental energy in whatever way it comes to them. This is where we begin to customize how we interact with energy. Some people may direct streams of colored light, others may summon rain storms, breathe fire, or dunk your recipients in a puddle of mud. The important goals for this exercise are that the healer gives their recipient(s) the energy they asked for and uses a method that feels right for them. This is how we learn our own unique techniques for healing.

Once you have selected roles and determined the kind of energy your recipient(s) wants to receive, sit at opposite sides of the room you are in. This journey takes place in the middle realm – the energetic counterpart to our physical world. In this journey, the healer will spirit walk across the room to direct energy to their recipient(s). If at any point in time the recipient needs the session to end, simply say 'STOP." Recipients should relax in a state of mindful awareness, taking note of any changes they feel.

Please use the 10 minute journey track located at blackfeathermystery.com/recordings or simply set a timer for 10 minutes. Remember, the intention for the Healer is to leave their body energetically, walk across the room, and direct the recipient's choice of energy into the recipient's energy body.

When you hear the callback part of the drum track, return to your body and then gently open your eyes. Give your partner(s) some feedback. Then, rotate roles and try the exercise again with different people as the healer and recipient(s). Remember to journal any experiences you wish to remember.

Individual Exercise

Select an object that will act as a reservoir into which you direct energy. Stones, bundles of herbs, and even living plants can all work well as recipients of energy. In this exercise, you will direct positive, life-giving energy to that object. Once you have selected an object and determined the kind of energy to use (earth, air, fire, water, or spirit), place the object at one end of the room and sit on the opposite side. This journey takes place in the middle realm – the energetic counterpart to our physical world. In this journey, you will spirit walk across the room to direct energy into the object.

Please use the 10 minute journey track located at blackfeathermystery.com/recordings or simply set a timer for 10 minutes. Remember, the intention for you is to leave your body energetically, walk across the room, and direct a particular elemental energy into the object.

When you hear the callback part of the drum track, return to your body and then gently open your eyes. Remember to journal any experiences you wish to remember.

Reflection

This exercise offers the opportunity to use some really fun metaphors to do beautiful work. Understand that on the back end of this GUI, you are using energies that contain universal information. We know our spirit bodies can be damaged. They can even be infected with parasites similarly to how your computer can get a virus. From a very science/tech standpoint, a spirit worker is basically the human equivalent of antivirus software. Doing energy work can be seen as running system updates, deleting unused programs to free up more space, and removing viruses from people. When our energy bodies are damaged, we seek energy from outside of us to repair it. Based on the holographic principle, we do this because all around us exists the energetic blueprint for the entire universe. That means our own energy is stored in there too, like backup copies of in the cloud. When we tap into the universe by focusing our minds into the theta wave state, we can then exert our will to re-download the information needed to fix issues in a person's etheric body. Your visualizations are your own custom GUI for handling all of that work.

BUILDING A TOOL BOX

This next journey is for you to continue fine tuning the way you interact with energy. You will go to your place of power and ask to be shown the following:

1. How do I channel the other four elements?
2. What are the best uses for channeling each one?

Please have your journal ready for this exercise. You may need to return occasionally to write things down, and then slip back into the journey. Consider also using this time to practice channeling all the elements. This is a longer journey. Please use the 15 minute journey track located at blackfeathermystery.com/recordings. Take your time, get as much information as possible, and experience your personal style of energy manipulation.

Going Forward

Journeying is a practice that is easy to pick up, but it can take a life-time to master all of its potential. Making a regular routine out of it is the best way to build the confidence and skills required to perform more and more advanced tasks. It is your chance to tap directly into the fabric of the universe and learn to wield it as a tool for great healing and progress. Every time you reconnect, you take another step towards claiming your power as a healer and spirit worker.

When you have finished your session, close the Ritual of Study as described on page 36.

CHAPTER TWELVE HOMEWORK

1. Practice the Blackfeather Self-Blessing, Grounding and Centering, and Shielding daily. Include five minutes of meditation, adding in an Elemental focus if so desired.
2. Continue your short divinatory practice, drawing one or two stones/cards/etc, and looking up the meanings of them. Remember, this is not a divination for the day. It is simply a way to help learn your divinatory tool's language.
3. Continue to explore Sacred Movement Practice. If you have a movement style that you enjoy, try to engage in it for a minimum of 10 minutes three times each week.
4. Journeywork: Continue your journeying practice using one of the journey audio tracks located at blackfeathermystery. com/recordings. You can use intentions for your journey from any previous chapter. Aim for three practice sessions per week.
5. Journaling Exercise: Begin your reflection, visioning and journaling process for the Fire section of Elemental Life Sculpting. Your entry should include answers to all of the questions in the Fire section of this class.

Additional Optional Journaling Exercises

Reflect on your experiences channeling elemental energy. Which was the easiest to channel? Which was the most challenging? What does that tell you about your own strengths?

Try to find someone willing to receive healing energy and practice healing energy work with them. Write down your experiences in your journal.

CHAPTER 13

THE LABYRINTH

For this chapter, you will need this book, your Blackfeather oil, your Blackfeather altar, a device that can play a recording online (if so desired), a card or small piece of paper, and your journal. This chapter includes a ritual that uses either a drawn or printed finger labyrinth (there are instructions for drawing one in the chapter) or a walkable labyrinth. If you plan to use a walkable labyrinth, read through this chapter during your study time, then perform the ritual later in the day or week when you can go to the labyrinth. Your instructor is Irene and this chapter should take two to three hours to go through.

B egin this chapter by performing the opening of the Ritual of Study on page 20.

THE LABYRINTH AS RITUAL TOOL

One of the simplest and most profound ritual tools I have ever encountered is a labyrinth. When used with intention and focus, these spiraling patterns have the power to transform, connect, and support us. One of the major turning points in my life occurred when I was in my late 20s. I was in the middle of a spiritual tailspin and the connection that I feel to the Divine and to the web of life around us (the same web we tap into during Blackfeather Grounding and Centering) had vanished for me. I was miserable, lost, and rapidly losing my sense of self.

I attended EarthSpirit's Twilight Covening retreat for the first time that year and studied with a group there that focused on labyrinth work. Before that day, I'd never walked a labyrinth or given them any thought. I left that retreat reconnected and firmly standing on the path that brought me here to you. I first became involved with my Unitarian Universalist congregation specifically because they have a labyrinth. I ran labyrinth walks long before I got involved with the pagan chapter at the congregation or became part of the fabric of congregational life.

To this day, when I feel lost or uncentered, I return to the labyrinth. Walking a labyrinth allows me to shortcut through my own nonsense to find the kernel of truth at the center, to reestablish communication with that which is greater than all of us, and to return refocused to my work in this world.

LABYRINTH OVERVIEW

In modern parlance, there is a difference between a Labyrinth and a Maze. A labyrinth is a geometric pattern that has a well-defined pathway winding to the center of the pattern and then back out again. It is a single path – there are no wrong turns or dead ends.

There are no decisions you need to make about where you are going on the labyrinth; it is not designed to confuse or bewilder you. In order to find the center of the labyrinth, all you have to do is follow your feet (or your finger for finger labyrinths). If you do happen to cross a line or get turned around, the worst thing that can happen is that you end up back at the beginning or visit the center of the labyrinth twice.

History

The oldest labyrinth patterns revealed to us through archeology date to a little over 5,000 years old. Some version of labyrinth appears in almost every culture in the world from, Crete to Ireland, the Middle East to Scandinavia and everywhere in between. They vary from culture to culture and are usually classified by the number of rings they have. That number varies from 3 to more than 11 depending on the labyrinth.

We do not know the reason for or origin of the oldest labyrinths and can only guess at their uses. Labyrinths are a 'lost' tradition. The largest, walkable ones, make the most sense as something humans would walk, dance, or crawl through. The ones carved into or painted onto walls, caves, and boulders may have had a symbolic meaning. No matter the culture, one thing seems to be true of labyrinths: they are consistently found in places that were considered sacred. The connection of labyrinths to spirituality, religion, or both appears to be universal.

When we see a concept repeated throughout the world regardless of language, culture, or history, we're looking at a piece of truth. We're seeing a slice of the collective unconscious that exists for all humans. The labyrinth is part of our spiritual DNA.

Contemporary Uses

The labyrinth as a spiritual tool is used as a way to find your center. Through moving back and forth toward the center of the pattern and away again, only to return finally to that space, we experience a physical metaphor for the journey to the sacred, centered Self. Labyrinths are used for meditation, reflection, prayer, healing, grieving, and problem solving. With intentional use and focus, labyrinths can help us shed issues, gain insight and cultivate wisdom. One of the interesting things about labyrinth walking in particular is that it is also used for community building. A group labyrinth walk is a solo spiritual practice we pursue in the company of others. It spans the gap between individual and communal experience.

The labyrinth is a large-scale allegory for the journey of life. Everything that happens during a walk contains a metaphor. For example, if we become impatient to reach the center, what does that tell us about our lives? If we stumble or become distracted, that can tell us a lot about our spiritual path. When we take to the labyrinth for the purpose of connecting, there are no mistakes or accidents. There's just meaning.

Finding a Labyrinth

The use of labyrinths for healing, meditation, and other spiritual practices have become more widespread and new labyrinths are regularly being constructed. They are often found at community centers, parks, congregations, and are becoming more common at hospitals. The easiest way to find a walkable labyrinth near you is to visit the World-Wide Labyrinth Locator online at https://labyrinthlocator.com. The Locator has been available since 2004 and is updated regularly with new labyrinths. Walkable labyrinths are my preferred form for labyrinth work, but finger labyrinths can also be effective. There are two printable finger labyrinths available for download through The Labyrinth Society at https://labyrinthsociety.org/download-a-labyrinth. The pattern I learned on and use most frequently is the Classical labyrinth, but all labyrinth patterns can be effective. Sculpted, carved, or otherwise three-dimensional labyrinths are commercially available. They can be more user-friendly than a printed labyrinth simply because you can then close your eyes while tracing the labyrinth and go deeper into meditation as a result.

Drawing a Labyrinth

To create your own labyrinth, drawing the Classical labyrinth pattern is easiest. Follow the graphics below to draw one. If you are creating a finger labyrinth, remember to keep a finger's space between the paths. If you are creating a walkable labyrinth with chalk, tape, or paint, the paths should be a minimum of 18" wide to allow for walking.

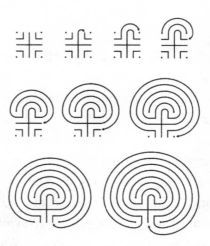

Figure 11: Diagram by Jonathan Morrow

USING THE LABYRINTH

There is just one rule to labyrinth use – there is no one right way to walk or trace a labyrinth. However, as with most tools for magick and spirituality, using the labyrinth for these purposes requires intention. Before you step onto the labyrinth, or begin to trace the pattern, take a moment to center yourself. A few deep breaths or Grounding and Centering (page 15) can help here. Allow your breathing to become slow and even. If you are walking a labyrinth, try to walk at a meditative pace – pay attention to the way your body is moving. There is no race to get to the center of the labyrinth. If you are tracing a labyrinth with your finger or a stylus, the same guidance applies. Go slowly and notice what you are feeling, physically, emotionally, and spiritually.

On a walkable labyrinth, it is acceptable to pass people. If someone is moving at a slow pace, it's totally fine to go around them. Likewise, if you sense people behind you, it's perfectly fine to step to the side to allow them to pass. Simply follow your feet as you walk. Remember that there's a single path to the center – as long as you follow that path, you'll end up there.

THE LABYRINTH RITUAL

There is a specific pattern that can be used when it comes to manifesting change through labyrinth walking. This is the practice that got me reconnected many years ago, and it remains the one I return to again and again. As you walk or trace a labyrinth, there are places where the path turns to face a different direction.

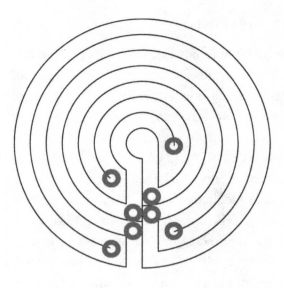

Figure 12: Turning Points on a Classic Labrinth

Each moment of change from one direction to another is an opportunity to change a perspective. Remember, everything that happens in a labyrinth is an allegory. So, to utilize those places on the labyrinth, we will follow a releasing-receiving pattern.

This labyrinth ritual is all about consecration. Your first, most powerful tool for magick is your Self – your sacred, magickal, powerful Self. Part of why we start Blackfeather with self-blessing is to empower you. Through this ritual, we will work on consecrating ourselves as spiritually empowered beings – as the vessels for magick that we truly are.

Visioning – Releasing – Receiving

Begin by visualizing yourself as you wish to be spiritually. You can return to the Guided Journey to the Mirror located on page 138 if you would find it helpful. Try to be as specific and detailed as possible with your visualization. Now, without judgment or punishment, consider what is standing in the way of manifesting that vision. Write down a list of the obstacles keeping you from that vision of yourself.

Now, looking at that list, figure out what hurdles and obstacles you can manifest some agency over. Some things are not negotiable - having a day job or parental responsibilities, for instance. But some things are: distraction, self-sabotage, self-doubt, fear, etc. Choose 3 to 5 obstacles that are workable – areas of your life where you have some agency.

Once you have selected those 3 to 5 obstacles, write down what you would replace them with. For instance, when I am working on developing more compassion through my labyrinth practice, I release "the need to be right," "control," and "fear." I replace those obstacles with "understanding," "community," and "love."

Putting it Together

On a card or small piece of paper, write down a consecration statement. This can be incredibly simple:

*'I consecrate myself as a divine being/vessel
for magick/empowered witch. So it is, so it shall be.'*

Feel free to use your own words here.

On the other side of the card or piece of paper, write down on the left half the 3 to 5 obstacles you are releasing. On the right half, write down the 3 to 5 blessings you are receiving – the blessings you are replacing those obstacles with.

You will need your card or piece of paper and your bottle of Blackfeather oil for this ritual. I will describe the ritual in two ways below: first using a walkable labyrinth, then using a traceable or finger labyrinth.

The Walkable Labyrinth Ritual

Center yourself before you walk into the Labyrinth. Set your intention. Then, on your journey to the center, focus on Releasing. At each point on the labyrinth, where you turn to face a different direction, pause and release one of the obstacles on your card. You will release all of them more than once. Also, if other things to release come up during the walk, feel free to follow those impulses. My preferred way to release something is to stop walking and use my hands to energetically 'push' that obstacle out of my body and into the earth.

When you reach the center of the labyrinth, softly speak or read your consecration statement to yourself. Using your oil, anoint yourself. Read the consecration statement again and say audibly, "So it is, so it shall be."

On your return journey from the center of the labyrinth, focus on Receiving. At each point on the labyrinth where you turn to face a different direction, pause and receive one of the blessings on your card. You will receive all of them more than once. And, again, if blessings come up that aren't written down, that's totally okay – go with it. My preferred way to receive a blessing is to stop and use my hands to draw that blessing up from the earth.

When you prepare to leave the labyrinth, pause one more time before stepping back out into consensus reality. Take a moment to notice how you feel. After stepping out of the labyrinth, turn to face the labyrinth and express gratitude to this sacred symbol. I do so by bringing my hands to my heart in prayer and bowing slightly. Then, write down anything you wish to remember about your experience, or any insights you have gained.

The Traceable/Finger Labyrinth Ritual

Gather your card or sheet of paper, your oil, and your finger labyrinth. Settle yourself before your Blackfeather altar. If you would like to, you are welcome to light incense or candles.

Center yourself prior to tracing the Labyrinth. Set your intention. Then, as you trace the path to the center, focus on Releasing. At each point on the labyrinth, where the path turns to face a different direction, pause and release one of the obstacles on your card. You will release all of them more than once. Also, if other things to release come up during this labyrinth work, feel free to follow those impulses. My preferred way to release something is to pause and mindfully exhale while visualizing releasing that obstacle out of my body.

When you reach the center of the labyrinth, softly speak or read your consecration statement to yourself. Using your oil, anoint yourself. Read the consecration statement again and say audibly, "So it is, so it shall be."

On your return journey from the center of the labyrinth, focus on Receiving. At each point on the labyrinth where the path turns to face a different direction, pause and receive one of the blessings on your card. You will receive all of them more than once. And, again, if blessings come up that aren't written down, that's totally okay – go with it. My preferred way to receive a blessing is to pause and mindfully inhale while visualizing that blessing arriving with my inhalation.

When you prepare to finish the labyrinth, pause one more time before completing the pattern. Take a moment to notice how you feel. After completing the labyrinth, express gratitude to this sacred symbol. I do so by bringing my hands to my heart in prayer and bowing slightly. Then, write down anything you wish to remember about your experience, or any insights you have gained.

Repetition

I perform this labyrinth ritual on most full moon nights of the year. In conjunction with Elemental Life Sculpting from Chapter Ten, it is an extremely effective way to support the work of empowerment and coming into your natural alignment. Try to make labyrinth use a regular part of your spiritual practice.

When you have finished your session, close the Ritual of Study as described on page 36.

CHAPTER THIRTEEN HOMEWORK

1. Practice the Blackfeather Self-Blessing, Grounding and Centering, and Shielding daily. Include five minutes of meditation.

2. Continue your short divinatory practice, drawing one or two stones/cards/etc, and looking up the meanings of them. Remember, this is not a divination for the day. It is simply a way to help learn your divinatory tool's language.

3. Continue to explore Sacred Movement Practice. If you have a movement style that you enjoy, try to engage in it for a minimum of 10 minutes three times each week.

4. Journeywork: Continue your journeying practice using one of the journey audio tracks located at blackfeathermystery. com/recordings. You can use intentions for your journey from any previous chapter. Aim for three practice sessions per week.

5. Journaling Exercise: Begin your reflection, visioning, and journaling process for the Water section of Elemental Life Sculpting. Your entry should include answers to all the questions in the Water section of that chapter.

6. Determine the location of the nearest labyrinths to you using the Worldwide Labyrinth Locator. If it is possible, plan to visit a few different ones in the coming months. If not, find a few different finger labyrinth patterns to try. Then, commit to a specific day for performing the Labyrinth Ritual roughly a month from now.

CHAPTER 14

EFFECTIVE SPELLCASTING

For this chapter, you will need this book, your Blackfeather oil, your Blackfeather altar, and a device that can play a recording online (if so desired). This chapter is lecture based. Your instructor is Irene and this chapter should take one to two hours to go through.

B egin this chapter by performing the opening of the Ritual of Study on page 20.

SPELLCRAFT AS A FORM OF AGENCY

Within a culture structured around obedience, conformity and hierarchy, one of the most powerful forms of rebellion is spellcraft. Witchcraft as an art form is the manipulation of reality in accordance with will – the ability to create desired change. Refusing to accept your situation and seizing power from the anonymous, impersonal forces that govern consensus reality is a way to reclaim agency in a world where our self-determination has been eroded.

There are reasons witches, cunning folk, root workers, seers, spirit workers and other magick wielders have been viewed as both resources and enemies at various points in history. People who are able to buck the system are scary. People who refuse to obey are problems. Moreover, many of us tend to inspire the people around us to behave similarly and one challenging witch can quickly become a social movement. This is why we've been burned, hanged, crushed to death, murdered in ten thousand ways, and still not destroyed. The witch spirit, the wild thread of magick that runs through the veins of some humans, is not something that can be wiped out. Our souls long for freedom, for self-determination. Witchcraft is one way we obtain those exact things.

One of the more amusing things I've discovered over the years is that although people claim not to believe in magick, when the shit really hits the fan, those same folks will seek out a witch to fix things. We are the last resort. We are what people turn to when all the rational, 'normal' ways of approaching a problem have failed. And the reason that still happens?

It's because magick works.

EFFECTIVE SPELLCASTING

But not always, of course. Some of that comes from a lack of under-standing about what makes an effective spell. A lot of the current spells we find in books and online are various types of positive thinking – visualize a goal, get it really solid in your mind, charge up a candle with that visualization and light it. Ta-da! Spell!

The problem is that good, solid spellcasting isn't that easy or simple. Like everything in magick, there are some good protocols to follow if you really want a spell to work. The practice of effective spellcasting can be seen as a series of steps.

Build the Base

It's tempting to just visualize a goal and light some incense, but most problems have real roots that exist for a reason. Situations don't just materialize out of the blue, at least not on the normal path of life. Understanding the current situation is absolutely vital because it will teach you what influences, energies and aspects of the situation *most need to be changed.*

Effective spellcasting requires a fair bit of journaling, and building the base is the first part you'll write down. Try to describe the current situation in detail. Start with the present situation, but then begin exploring what caused it to arise. I'll give you an example: let's say I want to do a spell to bring in money. My current situation might simply be not having enough money to pay my bills. The thing is, that lack didn't come out of nowhere. Maybe I work at a job that doesn't pay enough for the region I live in. Maybe I have bad spending and saving habits and have been abusing my credit cards. Maybe I've been hit with unexpected medical bills, major car repairs, or other unanticipated financial crises.

By understanding the situation more, we can begin to see what needs to move. A quick influx of money could fix a situation that is sudden and temporary like a car needing repairs. But if my need for money is part of a systemic problem – not making enough for my region, poor spending habits, or both – then the solution isn't a quick influx of cash. We've already learned more about what needs to move.

As you're journaling your base – your understanding of the situation – also consider what forces benefit from the situation remaining the same. Who or what benefits if nothing changes? Going back to my example, in this case it would be the forces of entropy and destruction, people who wish me ill and do not want me to succeed, people who benefit from paying me less than I am worth, and possibly people who benefit materially from me paying for more things than I can afford.

Design the Change

Just as you fully journaled a complete understanding of the current situation, envision and journal out a complete description of the situation as you would like it to be. And, just as in the previous journal entry, look for contributing factors in terms of environment and lifestyle that help support that desired change.

During the change portion of your journaling, explore what forces benefit from the situation changing. In this example, on a practical level, it would be me and my immediate family. On the energetic and divine levels, the forces would be those of Prosperity and Abundance. If you work with a particular pantheon, you'll begin to realize who your allies could be. Speaking as a Heathen, the deity I would see as a potential ally here is Freyr – the God most associated with abundance, prosperity, peace, and a good harvest.

The one thing to bear in mind as you design your change is to try not to describe how the transformation will occur. The Powers that Be have access to resources we do not, and frequently solve problems in surprising ways. You can, however, set parameters. For example, if you are casting a spell for an influx of cash, you can specify that it does not come from inheriting money due to the death of a loved one.

Break it Down and Seek Information

In complex situations, you may discover that your single spell for one particular situation really needs to be a few different spells spaced out over time. Breaking things into manageable chunks is a good idea. Using the first example, the very first spell might be getting a new job.

Figure out a timeline for the first steps. Spells with nebulous end times can take years to come to fruition. Look at your journal entry and figure out a small change that would support the complete vision that could occur within a month, or three months. Having that first little change go well is an indication that the spell is working. Minor adjustments like these make reflecting on the effectiveness of a spell after casting it easier.

At this point in your spell designing sequence, you should have a good understanding of the situation, a solid vision of where you want to go and what needs to change, and a rough timeline in mind. Now is a good time to consult your Spirits.

Journey to your Place of Power and ask to speak to a Guide. Sometimes there are additional obstacles in the way of a desired Change that we can't see from our point of view. Your Guides may have suggestions for additional changes that need to be made, or they may be able to support you in a way you had not anticipated. Occasionally, Guides will give instructions for a complete spell, which makes the next step a lot easier. That's an exception more than the rule, though. Note: if all your Guides and the humans you've talked about your plan with say it's a bad idea, you should listen to them.

After your Journey, write down all the information you received and begin to fit it into the larger picture of the spell.

Design the Spell

Here is where correspondence books and websites become useful. Figure out what colors, plants, minerals, planets, symbols, times/days and other correspondences support your Change. Determine what form your spell will take. The easiest and most user-friendly approach for beginning witches is to use an existing spell and adapt it to your specific needs. There are incredible compendiums of spells available commercially and vast collections of them available online, so I am not going to reinvent the wheel by including a collection of spells. However, there are some things to bear in mind when you are looking up a spell. The best spells include:

- A link to the desired outcome: a sigil or symbol, use of a focus drawing or photo that encapsulates your goal, building of an altar, or something else that connects you to the desired end result
- An action that generates energy: dancing or chanting, tapping into the energy of a strong natural source like the ocean or a healthy forest, accessing the power of an Element or Force like the sun, stars, wind or storms, or other energy-generating action
- A way to take that energy and convey it into the link: using your body to transfer the energy into the link through visualization, incantation, inscription or other action, or physically attaching the link to the power source (in the case of oceans, forests, fires, etc)

Feel free to change the wording in a spell that doesn't work for you. Add on and adjust where necessary. Remember the forces you are fighting against and consider including something to neutralize or appease them. Remember your potential allies and consider including a section of making offerings to them and requesting their help.

Plan three to five practical, real-world actions that will support your spell after you cast it. Dusting off a resume and applying for jobs is relatively straightforward. If your spell is for a friend who is desperately ill with a disease, these actions might be less obvious. Perhaps they involve starting a fundraiser for a research foundation, making food for that friend's family, or doing research on how best to support a loved one when they are struggling. Supporting the mechanism of a spell within the physical world helps create space for that energy to do its job.

It can sometimes help to remember that a good spell impacts all three layers of reality (spiritual, energetic, and physical) but that it is most impactful immediately to the spiritual and energetic layers. Physical reality is much denser. If we visualize a spell as falling rain, the 'rain' moves easily through the air – the energetic and spiritual layers. However, when it hits the ground, physical reality, things can be more complicated. A porous surface will accept the rain and the earth in that spot will be nourished. However, if the surface the rain hits is nonporous, no amount of 'water' will get through. By following a spell with physical change, we prepare the 'earth' to receive the 'rain' in a way that will be most helpful to us.

Perform the Spell

One brief caveat here – remember that spells work. Good spells work very well. Make sure you really want the change you've designed. Creating a spell that will heal your trauma may ultimately include events that bring that trauma to the surface for examining. The spell will work, but getting to the other side might involve some really challenging experiences. Also remember that the end goal you've visualized may come about in unexpected ways. If your choice of partner is the main reason you are stressed and you do a spell to reduce or eliminate the stress in your life, that partner may not be part of the picture going forward. Know what you want and understand what that change may involve.

- Clean. Tidy the area where you'll be performing the spell. Magick works best in harmonious environments that are not distracting or heavily cluttered. Clean yourself as well. For small spells, this can simply be washing your hands and face. For larger ones, a ritual shower or bath may be appropriate.
- Set up. Gather all the supplies you'll need and lay them out in a visually pleasing manner. This differs for everyone. I find it's useful to have a complete list of everything I need written down so that I don't forget anything. Include a divinatory tool (tarot, runes, oracle cards, etc) in your supply list for a confirmation divination. Remember to bring your journal and something to write with.
- Set the mood. If music, candlelight and incense help you feel more magickal, access all of those things. I personally dislike artificial light for magickal work.
- Protect the space. Cast a circle. You can also call on your Spirits to protect you here.
- Connect to your magickal self. For some people, this might involve a light trance state.
- Perform the spell.
- Get out your divination tool and ask if the spell was successful. Draw a single card, rune, ogham for your answer. If the draw indicates the answer is "no," ask what else needs to be done and perform another draw. Write down what those instructions are. If you can, follow them at this time. If not, plan to do so in the future. If you are having trouble determining what your divinatory tool is

trying to communicate, consider asking for help or doing a full reading on the subject later.

- Return to normal consciousness, ground and center. Eat something, or at least drink some water and rest a little to recover the energy you expended.
- Open the circle and clean up the space as necessary.
- The next day, begin working on the real-world actions that support the magick.

Evaluate your Work

As with all things magick, spellcraft techniques vary from person to person. We figure out what works for us through repetition and evaluation. This is similar to establishing a healthy diet – some of us are sensitive to tomatoes or peppers, some to dairy, some to wheat. Some of us do better with very little meat in our diets, some of us are closer to carnivores than anything else. We figure out what works by tinkering and observing the after-effects.

There is a tendency in some magickal circles to avoid reflecting on spells. I think for some people, it can feel blasphemous somehow. I suspect practitioners feel they are doubting the power and the will of the Universe/Gods/Whatever by examining how a spell went. The thing to remember is that witchcraft is an art and a science. This means a constant cycle of exploration and reflection. Witches get good at spells by doing them and figuring out what works and what does not.

I'm a big fan of calendar reminders. Set one for one month, three months and six months after casting the spell. Use this as an opportunity to reflect on how effective it was and record your reflections with that spell in your Book of Shadows, file, journal or whatever form of record you are keeping. Over time, you'll accumulate a great collection of spells that work well. Consider the following prompts when you're journaling out your evaluation of the spell.

- Did you see changes? If so, what form did they take?
- How long did the spell take to start working? Did it work completely, or improve the situation?
- In retrospect, if you had known how the spell was going to manifest, would you have changed anything?
- Did you discover any additional obstacles preventing the spell from working thoroughly? Are they things you can remove?

Journey to consult with your spirits about the spell. They have resources, information and connections we do not, and may be able to give you feedback you could not see from your perspective. Include their feedback with your own.

Sometimes spells fail. There are a few different reasons this can happen. The one big, unchangeable one is referred to by author Christopher Penczak as 'Not for you.' Occasionally, no matter how much power, thought, visualization and effort we put into a spell, it will not work. The outcome we desire is, for whatever reason, not open to us right now. This is also true for overcoming obstacles that are too powerful and entrenched to be influenced. An example of that would be trying to heal someone with a terminal diagnosis. Try, by all means. Sometimes we can influence the worst situations, even if it's just to slow the oncoming train down a little, or ease a person's passage into the next life. But also understand that some forces are damn near unstoppable. There is a very real matter of leverage when it comes to spellcraft. The best straw in the world will not be enough to lift a car.

Many times, however, the reason a spell fails has nothing to do with the will of the Powers That Be or the obstacle you're trying to overcome. If a spell failed, look at the spell closely. Was the visualization specific enough? Realistic enough? Did you put enough power into the spell? If you used a spell someone else wrote, is it just not right for you? It might be good to try a different spell.

Spells can be repeated and improved upon. If your first pass wasn't effective, or wasn't as effective as you'd like it to be, improve your design and try again. If you are consistently met with total spell failure, the goal you're working on falls into the category of 'Not for you.'

USE YOUR MAGICK

I know a shocking number of Pagans who do not use magick or do spellcraft. Some people really do just enjoy the devotional and mythical aspects of Pagan practice. But witches? Witches cast spells. Witches do magick. You have the capacity within you to create change – real change – in your life and in the world around you. Use it.

When you have finished your session, close the Ritual of Study as described on page 36.

CHAPTER FOURTEEN HOMEWORK

1. Practice the Blackfeather Self-Blessing, Grounding and Centering, and Shielding daily. Increase to seven minutes of meditation.

2. Continue your short divinatory practice, drawing one or two stones/cards/etc, and looking up the meanings of them. Remember, this is not a divination for the day. It is simply a way to help learn your divinatory tool's language.

3. Continue to explore Sacred Movement Practice. If you have a movement style that you enjoy, try to engage in it for a minimum of 10 minutes three times each week.

4. Journeywork: Continue your journeying practice using one of the journey audio tracks located at blackfeathermystery. com/recordings. You can use intentions for your journey from any previous chapter. Aim for three practice sessions per week.

5. Journaling Exercise: Begin your reflection, visioning, and journaling process for the Spirit section of Elemental Life Sculpting. Your entry should include answers to all the questions in the Spirit section of that chapter.

6. Journaling Exercise: Consider what situations around you might be improved through spellcraft. Choose one area to work on and begin designing the spell for it following the guidance in this chapter.

CHAPTER 15

TEMPLE ARTS

*For this chapter, you will need this book, your Blackfeather
oil, your Blackfeather altar, a device that can play a
recording online (if so desired), your journal, and your
partner if you are working with one. The exercise in this
chapter can also be performed solitary. This chapter is
lecture based and includes one exercise.
Your instructor is Irene and this chapter should take two to
three hours to go through.*

B egin this chapter by performing the opening of the Ritual of
Study on page 20.

MYSTERY, TRANSCENDENCE, AND RITUAL

People do not end up exploring Paganism by accident. It's not a
belief system one falls backward into. If you are holding this book,
it's because you're looking for something. For most people, that

nebulous something is a form of connection – a transcendental experience with a power larger than ourselves. The name that power goes by varies between practitioners, but for many of us those moments of connection are what keep us on this path.

Religions are containers for Mystery. They are designed to hold the experience of transcendence and give their practitioners a framework with which to put a revelatory experience into context. Not every container will fit every transcendent experience. Some of the most common religious containers in Western culture do not allow for the experiences that Pagans have. Encountering the earth as sentient, connecting with the Spirits, communicating with the Gods, and psychic phenomena are frequently not a part of mainstream religions.

People need Mystery. What I hear most frequently from folks exploring this path is that the religion they came from feels empty to them. Many people will stay with a belief system for the social benefits but lack any sense of spiritual connection. The thing is, spiritual experiences are part of what keeps us going. They help us know we are a part of a greater tapestry. They reassure us when things go horribly wrong, help us stay centered and grounded when things go right, and give us a thread to hold as we navigate the maze that is the human experience.

Rituals, at their very best, hold space for a transcendental experience to occur. If a religion is the macrocosm, ritual is the microcosm. Just as a religion holds the mystery in a particular way, so too do rituals. As with religions, the shape and style of rituals matter. They are oriented toward particular types of experiences. What is moving and transcendental for one practitioner may not be for another. This is why you can go to a pagan public ritual with a friend and feel nothing but have your friend come out wide-eyed and changed.

Despite that variation, there are some good general guidelines for creating and facilitating ritual experiences that foster transcendental experiences. The most beautifully dressed ritual with the fanciest candelabra accomplishes nothing without content.

RITUALS AND SPELLS

What is a ritual? In common parlance, it's any action that is repeated regularly in a particular order. The way you brush your teeth in the morning is a daily ritual. However, for the purposes of this session, I am going to use the word "ritual" to mean a pre-designed ceremony with the goal of connection, spellwork, or worship.

A spell is the pre-designed raising and direction of energy to cause a specific outcome (basically everything in Chapter Fourteen). Sometimes the line between a ritual and a spell can get a little blurry. Very elaborate spells can include many traits of rituals, and folks will frequently use the same word to reference both kinds of Workings. The determining factor here is where the energy is going – what is the Work at the center of the ritual? If it is to effect change on the physical plane, you are doing a spell. If it is to foster a transcendental experience, to offer worship or praise to a Power, it is a ritual.

Pagan High Holidays

In contemporary pagan practice, we visualize the year as a wheel with eight points – the High Holidays. At two points on the wheel are the solstices – the times of greatest daylight and greatest darkness. In the middle of those points on both sides of the wheel are the equinoxes – the time of balanced day and night that occur each spring and fall. These four holidays are sometimes referred to as the quarters. In between each solstice and equinox is a cross-quarter day, a holiday marking the midpoint of the transition.

There are variations on the high holidays within different practices of paganism. The list below is an overview of the holidays as generally accepted in wider pagan tradition.

Yule: The Winter Solstice Yule marks the shortest day and longest night of the year. It generally falls around the 21st or 22nd of December. On Yule, we welcome the return of the sun, knowing that from this point till the summer solstice, the days will grow longer.

Imbolc: The Winter Cross-Quarter Imbolc marks the halfway point between the winter solstice and the spring equinox. We observe it on February 1st. On Imbolc, we celebrate the early signs of the spring to come. This holiday is also frequently interpreted as a time of purification.

Ostara: The Spring Equinox Ostara falls on the spring equinox – the day of equal light and darkness. It is the official start of springtime and generally falls on March 21st or 22nd. On Ostara, we celebrate the new life emerging from its winter sleep.

Beltane: The Spring Cross-Quarter Beltane marks the halfway point between the spring equinox and the summer solstice. On Beltane, we celebrate and revel in the growth and fertility of the natural world as spring starts transitioning to summer. Beltane is celebrated on May 1st and often includes themes of romantic love.

Litha: The Summer Solstice Litha marks the longest day and shortest night of the year. It generally falls around the 21st or 22nd of June. On Litha, we honor the abundance around us and celebrate the bounty brought by abundant sunlight.

Lughnassadh: The Summer Cross-Quarter Lughnassadh (also sometimes called Lammas) falls at the midpoint between the summer solstice and the autumnal equinox. It is the first of our three harvest holidays and marks the grain harvest. Lughnassadh is celebrated on August 1st.

Harvest Home: The Autumnal Equinox Harvest Home (also sometimes called Mabon) falls on the autumnal equinox – the day of equal light and darkness. It is the official start of autumn and generally falls on September 21st or 22nd. Harvest Home is the second of our three harvest holidays and marks the vegetable harvest. It is often referenced as 'Pagan Thanksgiving' and is frequently celebrated with feasting.

Samhain: The Autumn Cross-Quarter Samhain falls at the midpoint between the autumnal equinox and the winter solstice. It marks the last harvest – the harvest of gourds and tubers, but also the culling of herds. Samhain marks the transition from a season of growth to a season of rest, death, and rebirth. It is a time when we honor our ancestors and prepare for the winter to come. Samhain falls on October 31st and is the most widely-known of the pagan high holidays.

THE RITUAL TRIAD

The ability to create effective rituals – ceremonies designed to foster transcendental experience – is a skill set, and one that improves with practice and experience. However, there are some good guidelines you can follow. The best rituals contain The Ritual Triad: Emotion, Visualization and Action.

Emotion

Humans are, for the most part, emotional creatures. Our emotions color and frequently govern our thoughts and experiences. Personal energy is also tied to emotion. Think about the sharp rush of adrenaline you experience when you feel fear, or the heat and shaking when you feel anger, or the breathless wonder you experience at heartbreakingly beautiful sights. When we approach ritual design, finding a way to engage our emotions and the emotions of the other participants is the first step. By speaking to the emotional truth of a ceremony, we engage the energy, incentive and investment of all the participants. It is easier to raise energy if we feel personally connected to and invested in the emotions at the center of any Working.

Visualization

Along with accessing our energy through emotion, rituals need a visualization – a framework to hold the emotion and ritual actions. The visualization is frequently supported by stagecraft aspects of ritual design. It's easy to envision oneself in the Underworld, or standing just this side of the Veil between life and death when one is in front of a giant altar covered in black candles, photographs, and sacred objects.

Visualizations can also be simple and require very little set dressing. We can visualize a beam of light connecting us to the earth, stars, or sun. We can visualize ourselves visiting the Temple or Hall of one of the Powers. We can visualize mist rising from the earth, flames surrounding us, or an ocean appearing at our feet.

Action

The ritual action is a physical embodiment of the emotion and visualization. It's what we do to take those emotions, couple them with a visualization, and get the energy of that experience to its intended recipient. Ritual actions can take the form of:

- Communication or Communion with a Power: a Journeywork or Possessory piece
- Example: Journeying to the Hall or Temple of a God to receive a message, visualizing ourselves in the company of a Power, trance possession (not to be attempted by beginners, please)
- Offering worship or praise: prayers, litanies, sacred poetry, chants, songs
- Example: Performing a chant written in praise of a God, singing to the land spirits, prostration to a Power
- Gifting: offering an energetic or physical gift to the Power you are working with
- Example: Pouring libations, dedicating a particular object to that Power, sending energy to a specific Power

FINDING THE KERNEL

When I approach ritual design, the first thing I find is the kernel of the ritual – a center point that allows me to use the Triad to flesh out the ritual. The kernel is a single word to three-word phrase that encapsulates the deepest truth of that ritual. Kernels are generally simple. The best, most profound rituals come from a place of simplicity.

To find the kernel, start with the myths around the ritual or Power. For example, if you're creating a seasonal ritual like any of the

Pagan high holidays, read stories and folklore about that point in the year. If you're creating a ritual for a specific Path or God, read the myths about that Being.

Using what you understand about the myths, determine the emotional truth of the ritual. An easy example is Samhain. The myths around Samhain are that it is the witches' new year, that it's the time when the Veil between the living and dead is thinnest, that is the beginning of the season of Death. The folk practices include dumb (silent) suppers, divination, and ancestral offerings.

If we take a step back and really distill Samhain, the emotional truth of the holiday is *grief.*

This distillation process should be considered for feast days, holidays, Rites of Passage, and any other ritual you plan to design and perform. The kernel you discover then informs how the ritual takes shape.

RITUAL SIZE

The larger the group participating in the ritual, the simpler the actions need to be and fewer actions need to occur. This is part of why finding the kernel of a ritual can be so important. If you understand the deepest truth of why a ritual is happening, you'll be able to address that truth whether your ritual includes 2 people or 200 people.

If you are designing for a group, remember that people have a finite amount of emotional and psychological energy to expend. Everyone still needs to be able to drive home after a ritual. Also, profound experiences require space and focus. Having too much 'stuff,' too many chants, actions or activities, distracts from that experience. Build beauty around simplicity.

If you are working with a group of under 10 people, you can have as many ritual actions as the group can understand/execute. I had a working partner for many years and our Imbolc ritual every year was based around purification. It included sacred bathing, a crystal grid energy attunement, anointing...it was really elaborate. Something with that many supplies and steps can work for a group that numbers less than 10.

Groups up to 20 in number can include up to 5 actions or activities based on the skill level of that group. Groups larger than 20 should max out at 3 ritual actions or activities. If your group is varied in age and experience, those actions should be understandable by a child.

In order to create a space that supports transcendental experience, all people present should be active participants in the Work of the ritual. There's an unfortunate tendency in much of modern pagan ritual for performance rather than participatory ritual. Watching other people do a ritual rarely triggers a profound religious experience for the individual observing.

SACRED THEATER

Our emotions and subconscious respond to nonverbal cues. They respond to tone, appearance, music, rhythm, movement, light levels, color and shape. One of the easiest illustrations of this is the power of light. When a room is filled with fluorescent light, the mood we feel is very practical. It's an environment for learning, mundane work, and logical, linear activity. When we light that exact same room with candles, regardless of how industrial the room is, suddenly the space feels intimate and mysterious. The possibility of Mystery becomes more likely.

Sacred Theater is the art of creating the correct space and tone of a ritual. Just as a ritual performed in a bright, fluorescently lit room will most likely fall flat, a ritual performed in a sensorily evocative space is more likely to induce a transcendental experience.

Remember that performance does not equal pretending. Knowing what you are going to say or do ahead of time leaves *more* space for the speaker to experience or channel connection simply because that individual isn't thinking about what comes next or scrambling to find the right words. Sacred performance allows us to express and transfer what we experience in direct communion with a Power to what others can see and experience on the outside of that exchange. When I am deep in communion with a Power, it doesn't look like much on the outside. In order to share that connection, I must give sound, movement, posture, words, or other sensory forms to that experience.

Sacred Performance, like ritual creation, is a set of skills that improve and evolve over time. Again, there are some good basic guidelines to work from.

Stance and Gesture

Humans read a lot into how an individual stands and moves. When you are reading an invocation, litany of praise, or any spoken part in a ritual, think about what stance or movements embody the words you are saying. Think of this like interpretative dance – how can your body say the same thing as your words?

Memorization

If you are not trying to read in flickering light or struggling with coming up with what to say next, you are free to channel energy through you and use Sacred Theater techniques. You can open up to the Power you are communicating with, invoking, or worshipping. You can move your body freely since you're not holding a script. Moreover, stumbling over invocations, instructions or chants can knock the energy right out of a ritual. It breaks the aesthetics of the container. Memorization is a wonderful support for Sacred Theater.

Some tricks for memorization: rhyming poetry is easier to memorize than prose. Break what you are memorizing into smaller chunks. I like to focus on three to four lines at a time. Even if you plan to speak rather than sing a spoken part, fit a melody to whatever it is you're trying to memorize. We recall songs with even more ease than things that rhyme but are not melodic.

Have a cheat sheet. As useful as memorization is, it's not uncommon to blank suddenly in the midst of a meaningful ritual. Invest in a nice three-ring binder so that your ritual script is not just a stack of paper or cards that you are shuffling through. Print your ritual out in large, thick font so that it's easy to see even if the light is low. Put the ritual in the binder and have it on hand, just in case.

Ritual Voice

Our voices are one of the most versatile tools we have. A voice can set the tone of a particular space or action and help control the flow of energy. Voices can serve as a point of focus. Most importantly, our voices are malleable: they can be shifted in pace, tone and volume to reflect different energies, Powers and emotions. Our voices are used for both invocations and offerings. A well-delivered invocation is both an invitation and a gift.

Speed: Remember that you need to leave space for people to process fully what you are saying. Nervousness increases speed. A good general guideline is to try to speak at half your normal rate.

Tone: We speak on a melody, whether or not we are conscious of it. Pay attention to the melody of your speech. Sentences that end on a higher note sound like questions. When guiding an activity, ending sentences on a question-sound causes people to feel less secure. They begin to doubt that the speaker is fully confident. When you are giving instructions, guiding the flow of energy, or acting as a stable presence in a ritual, end your sentences on a lower note.

Volume: The softer you speak, the more people have to strain to listen. Sometimes this is good. Forcing active listening at certain points can help strengthen the focus of a group. However, always be aware of folks with auditory limitations. More than anything, a speaker should be able to be heard by an entire assembled group.

Emphasis: When you are looking at a spoken part for a ritual, circle or highlight the words you wish to emphasize.

Elemental Voice

When I am choosing how to use my voice for Sacred Theater, I look to the Elements. Each Element has a specific way to express their energy vocally.

Earth voice is low, slow, and steady. The melody of the voice stays toward the low register. Words are delivered firmly and clearly. Earth voice is a good choice for guided meditations, calming and focusing people.

Air voice is slow but spacious and open. The melody of the voice is higher in the register. For Air voice, add breath to your voice. It has the quality of a whisper but the volume of full voice.

Fire voice is sharp. It is faster paced but not rushed. Fire voice is forceful and passionate. Emphasize the closing consonants of words. The melody of the voice is driving. It can elevate a little at the end of sentences, but not enough to indicate a question.

Water voice is low, slow and flowing. Vowels and consonants can be more sustained. The melody of the voice moves around a lot within the register. This change in melody is what most separates Water voice from Earth voice.

Spirit voice is higher pitched. We send the voice forward toward the nasal cavity without treading into a squeaky or droning sound. Spirit voice is inspired and flowing. There's a little bit of breath on the voice and a sense of spaciousness.

Elemental Voice Exercise

A recording of the examples below is available at blackfeathermystery.com/recordings. Using the guidance above, or by listening to the example first, practice saying the paragraphs below using Elemental voice. If you are working with a partner or a small group, take turns and give each other constructive feedback. If you are working by yourself, you can consider recording your voice onto a device and listening back to notice how each Element manifests in your words.

Earth: The basis and foundation of all the elements is the Earth. The Earth is the object; subject and receptacle of all celestial rays and influences and in it are the seeds of all things. It is made fruitful by the other elements and the heavens, and brings forth all things of itself. It is the first fountain whence all things spring; it is the center, foundation and mother of all things. Earth is the element of stability, foundations, and the body. The Earth is the realm of wisdom, knowledge, strength, growth, and prosperity. It is also the physical Earth on which we live and the very heart of life.

Air: The element of Air is vital to human survival; without it we would all perish. Air is the manifestation of movement, freshness, communication, and intelligence. Sound is another manifestation of this element. Air is the power of the mind, the force of intellect, inspiration, imagination. It is ideas, knowledge, dreams and wishes. Air is the element of new life and new possibilities and is essential to spells and rituals of travel, instruction, finding lost items, some types of divination, and freedom. It is the vital spirit passing through all things, giving life to all things, moving and filling all things.

Fire: The element of Fire is both creative and destructive. It is fire that we and our ancestors used to warm our homes; we use it to cook our food; we sit around it to ward off the darkness of night, and it fuels our passions. Fire is the transformer, converting the energy of other objects into other forms: heat, light, ash, and smoke. Fire contains the aspects of change, passion, creativity, motivation, will power, drive, and sensuality. It is sexuality, both physical and spiritual. Fire is used in spells, rituals, and candle magic for healing, purification, sex, breaking bad habits, or destroying illness and disease. Fire is the element of authority and leadership.

Water: Water is a cleansing, healing, psychic, and loving element. It is the feeling of friendship and love that pours over us when we are with our family, friends and loved ones. When we swim, it is water that supports us. When we are thirsty, it is water that quenches our thirst. Another manifestation of this element is the rainstorms that drench us, or the dew formed on plants after the sun has set. You can feel its cool liquidity; its soft and loving touch. As well as being vital for life, within the energy of this element is contained the essence of love. Love is the underlying reason for all magic. Water is love.

Spirit: Spirit is the binding force between the other elements that runs through all matter, and is the collective unconscious of life-forms. The word itself is Persian and means "inner space." The Elements emerge from Spirit, the immutable, changeless source of all energy. This is the realm of potentiality: of promise, of paths not yet taken, of unformed galaxies, of outer space. Spirit is also present within our bodies as the spark of life, the mystical force that is called the soul. The energy of Spirit, which extends everywhere throughout the universe, is constantly creating form and substance. It's the primal source of energy that creates and fuels all that is.

CREATING AND SELECTING SACRED LANGUAGE

When you are writing the spoken portions of a ritual, choose evocative language. Use words and phrases that describe the energy you are accessing or the deity you are invoking in a flattering way. Remember that particularly with Gods, you can emphasize different aspects based on the way you would like to approach that deity. For example, the Norse goddess Freyja is both a sorceress and a warrior. How you speak about and to her will influence the energy of a ritual for her.

Use language that helps people imagine the forces you are calling:

> The rocks and stones that dwell in darkness at the root of the mountain
> The breeze that whips through the valley, stirring leaves to dance in its passing
> The crackling flame that breaks through the darkness, sparking light and hope
> The flowing stream that pours down the cliffs, meandering to end in the deep ocean

Last, *practice*. Speak your part out loud. Experiment with your voice. Find the right expression for that particular aspect of the ritual. When you put it all together, your rituals will connect more deeply with the participants in them.

When you have finished your session, close the Ritual of Study as described on page 36.

CHAPTER FIFTEEN HOMEWORK

1. Practice the Blackfeather Self-Blessing, Grounding and Centering, and Shielding daily. Increase to seven minutes of meditation.

2. Continue your short divinatory practice, drawing one or two stones/cards/etc, and looking up the meanings of them. Remember, this is not a divination for the day. It is simply a way to help learn your divinatory tool's language.

3. Continue to explore Sacred Movement Practice. If you have a movement style that you enjoy, try to engage in it for a minimum of 10 minutes three times each week.

4. Journeywork: Continue your journeying practice using one of the journey audio tracks located at blackfeathermystery. com/recordings. You can use intentions for your journey from any previous chapter. Aim for three practice sessions per week.

5. Journaling Exercise: Return to the 'Your First Sculpt' section of Chapter Ten (on page 153) and for each Element write out a few simple, small steps you can take to begin bringing your life into alignment there.

6. Journaling Exercise: Choosing one of the Pagan high holidays other than Samhain, determine the kernel of one of the following: Yule, Imbolc, Ostara, Beltane, Litha, Lammas, or Harvest Home.

7. Journaling Exercise: If you have attended rituals before, write down which ones you enjoyed and why. What stood out about the ritual? What experiences there inspired you?

CHAPTER 16

DEVOTIONAL WITCHCRAFT

*For this chapter, you will need this book, your Blackfeather
oil, your Blackfeather altar, a device that can play a
recording online (if so desired), and your journal. This
chapter includes some journeywork, so a comfortable place
to sit where you will be relaxed but not in danger of falling
asleep can be useful. Your instructor is Irene and this
chapter should take two to three hours to go through.*

B egin this chapter by performing the opening of the Ritual of
Study on page 20.

The Blackfeather style of witchcraft places focus on cocreative, relationship-based magick. This style is sometimes referred to
as Devotional Witchcraft. It hinges on devotion to and cultivation of
our connection to other Beings – spirit allies, noncorporeal spirits,
spirits of place, and, of course, Gods.

GEOGRAPHY AND RELATIONSHIPS

My best friend is a self-described desert rat. She lives in Arizona in the western United States and has done so for most of her life. One of the first times I went to visit her, we went on a bike ride. As we were coming around a path in a park, I saw a snake sunning itself on the trail. Now, I'm from Maryland in the east coast United States. Here, snakes are benign for the most part. The handful of poisonous snakes in our region is low and we certainly don't find them in a park in the middle of a suburban area. So I didn't slow down – I planned to ride past the snake. My friend began to holler and yell at me to stop. So, I turned back to her.

The snake in the middle of the path was a rattlesnake. My best friend knew that a more dangerous snake was likely because that region is her home.

When a snake appears in a dream or as part of a reading, I view them as messengers of transformation – of shedding that which no longer serves. If a snake appears in a dream or as part of a reading where my best friend is concerned, she sees them as a threat.

A witch's relationship to their immediate geographical surroundings, to their home, plays a huge part in correspondences. How we feel about the local fauna and flora determines what those friendships and alliances are like. I'm not sure about the origin of this phrase, but the saying "a witch should intimately know the five miles surrounding their home," rings very true. We are earthy beings, connected to the land and spirits around us. In a workshop at Sacred Space Conference in 2019, author and teacher John Beckett described regional Paganism: allowing our beliefs to vary by region. He said that Paganism should be the intersection of the Ancestors, the Gods and the physical space in which we live and practice.

In previous chapters, we focused on the Elements and Elementals. Relationships with the Elementals are useful for correspondences because they are a shortcut to interacting with any Being under the purview of one of the Elementals. As an example, say you want to use amethyst as part of a working but haven't cultivated a relationship with amethyst yet. By reaching out to Elemental Earth (who you already have a relationship with), you can establish a friendship with amethyst more quickly.

In this class, we are going to focus on working with the gnars/egregores/overspirits of particular kinds of Beings. We'll be exploring how to begin, sustain and honor those relationships.

LOCALLY SOURCED MAGICK

Once upon a time, humans were an integral part of the small ecosystems in which they lived. Everything we consumed was harvested locally whether that was meat, vegetables, grain, fruit, or medicine. Our waste was likewise disposed of locally – it went back into the ground to be broken down and turned into resources for new life. When our bodies died, they were also buried locally. We literally returned to the land that sustained our lives. The energy of our specific region permeated us.

The movement toward local food is a great thing to see. No matter what, we depend upon the land and its Beings in order to survive. Doing so responsibly and sustainably supports a better relationship. By making that relationship local, we bring the benefits home. Making our very cells and bodies part of the relationship with the local Beings is a powerful way to enhance our metaphysical working relationships with them.

This philosophy of local sourcing applies to spell, ritual, and working ingredients. There are giant compendiums of metaphysical correspondences not to mention multiple websites devoted to the subject. However, those correspondences tend not to be listed by region. When you are working magick, your magick carries the blessing of other beings who work with you and your strongest relationships will be with local spirits.

Although it's tempting to have a magickal cabinet filled with herbs and crystals from all over the world, I would invite you to consider sourcing local supplies. Farmer's markets and co-ops are great places to find fresh herbs grown locally. Even if a species isn't native to your region, if it's grown there it is part of the regional tapestry of spirits. This functions similarly to emigration – just because our ancestors aren't from this country doesn't mean we can't have deep and meaningful relationships with the local spirits. By living where we do, we become part of the tapestry.

Many herbs have multiple metaphysical correspondences. Let's use Rosemary as an example. It's commonly grown in my region, although it needs to be brought indoors during winter. Rosemary is associated with purification, strength, protection, energy, memory, and sun. What multiple correspondences per herb means in a practical sense is that you could cultivate relationships with 15 to 20 locally grown kinds of plants and be able to do almost any kind of correspondence-assisted magick as a result.

This is also true of stones and crystals. Different crystals are common in different regions. Where I live in western Maryland, quartz, mica, garnet, and feldspars (moonstone, labradorite, etc) are common. However, the world of mineral magick doesn't stop at the sparkly rocks. Stones are minerals too and all carry different qualities. A piece of Catoctin Greenstone – the greenish-tinted metabasalt common to the mountains where I live – resonates with ancient, stable energy. It would be a good ally in any magick involving abundance, stability, safety and protection. Learn about the geology where you live. If you see an interesting rock, look it up. You'd be amazed at the allies around you that go overlooked because they aren't sparkly.

Consider expanding your understanding of correspondences to favor local beings. Choose plants and flowers that grow near you. Work with stones and crystals that live with you. If you have the ability to do so, grow some herbs that you use regularly at your house. Think of correspondences not as a user agreement, but as a long-term friendship with your spirit-neighbors.

CULTIVATING RELATIONSHIPS

There are a couple of different ways to approach building a relation-ship with a being you'd like to work with. You can approach the gnar or you can approach the individuated being. As mentioned in Chapter Two, a gnar or overspirit is the collective governing energy being for a particular species or gathered group. Just as all cells in a human body are part of that specific human, all individual daffodils are part of the daffodil gnar. If you are planning to work with a correspondence that will be combined with individual beings – think locally sourced lavender oil or a group of quartz crystals – approaching the gnar to form the relationship will be the most useful and least time-consuming option.

An individuated being is the specific crystal, herb, tree, or body of water you want to work with. There are times when approaching an individuated being is the most useful path. A long-term spell using one specific stone or crystal is a good example.

First Contact

Relationship building with spirits is not so different from making friends with people. Healthy friendships are built on respect, shared interest and balanced energy exchange. Establishing contact with a particular spirit can follow a simple path:

Journey to meet the spirit. It is easier to connect on a spiritual level when we are in a mental state conducive to spirit communication. As your relationship with a particular spirit becomes stronger, you may not need this step, but it's a good place to begin. Plan to set aside at least 20 minutes for a mediation. Settle yourself comfortably, then rattle, drum or play an appropriate track in the background for journeying. Background journey tracks can be found at blackfeathermystery.com/recordings. Start in a place of safety - your landing pad or place of power. Invite the spirit you wish to communicate with to join you there. If they cannot do so, travel to meet them instead.

Offer a gift. Thank the spirit for being willing to meet with you. Offer them a gift of some sort in gratitude for their time and energy. I like to make beautiful energy structures – crystals, flowers, spheres of light – and then offer them. To do so, simply gather up some of your own energy. Start with an energy ball and then, using visualization, shape it into the form you would like to offer.

Explain your goals. Tell the spirit why you're calling on them. Explain what kind of magick you're working on and how a successful working will impact your life.

Request assistance. Ask if the spirit would be willing to work with you on your goal. If they are, ask what form would work best.

Offer assistance. If the spirit agrees to work with you, ask what you can do to support them in return. Be honest about what you're willing to do as part of this relationship.

Determine the path forward. If you decide to work together, talk about the shape that will take. If you're planning to grow a mugwort plant to help make your home energetically invisible, decide where that plant will be located and discuss what it needs in order to thrive.

Part as friends. Express gratitude and affection and return. Write down the contents of your journey. Once we reenter normal cognitive space, it's easy to lose bits and pieces.

Sustaining the Relationship

Friendships can take different forms in terms of how long they last. Some friendships are formed for a reason – anyone who has gone on a retreat, to a convention, or on a vacation as part of a tour group understands friendships that are specific to one particular location or situation. Some friendships last longer – a season. These are the friendships we form with classmates in school. We sit next to the same people for 6 months or a year and develop relationships that sustain that time period. Some friendships last years or longer. These are relationships that include shared goals and visions, common experiences and deep affection and connection.

Your working relationships with correspondences will have similar variation. Some will last longer than others. All friendships take some effort to sustain. In the case of a living plant, that can be as simple as tending it – watering, weeding and visiting. For a longer term relationship, it might mean regular journeys to check in with your ally. Remember that when you start a friendship, if you wish to be able to ask for help later, you need to maintain the friendship. This is just like human friendships – we all dislike the person who only talks to us when they need something.

Acting as an ally toward the gnar of a species you're working with can be really helpful, too. As an example, let's say you're working with a barred owl as a way to overcome fear of the dark. You can support barred owls in your region by donating to or volunteering at wildlife sanctuaries they call home. This is equally true of supporting the allies of that being. If you live in an apartment or don't do well growing your own herbs, purchasing plant material from local growers is a great way to support that particular species.

EXERCISE: STARTING A RELATIONSHIP

Think about a goal you're working on. Using the internet or any correspondence texts you may already own, look up a plant, animal, bird, or mineral that supports that kind of work. Try to choose a being that lives or can live in your region. Once you have selected that being, look at some photos of it online so that you're familiar with its appearance.

When you have finished, journey to meet the being you are seeking a connection with. Please use the ten-minute journey track located at blackfeathermystery.com/recordings. In this journey, you can return when your conversation has finished. However, if you hear the callback – the change in rhythm and volume – it's definitely time to return.

Your intention to repeat three times is:

"I invite the spirit of _____ to meet me in my Place of Power."

Once you get back, write down your experience.

THE SPIRIT COURT

Over the course of many years, a witch practicing devotional or relationship-based witchcraft gathers to themselves a host of connections. Some of these relationships are closer than others – we may work with a primary spirit guide, ancestor or deity more than other contacts. Thinking of one's Spirit Court as being similar to a social circle is useful. You'll have some connections that are part of your innermost circle – beings you may be in daily contact with. You'll also cultivate connections that are cordial, respectful and friendly, but are more distant. Think of these connections as being like friends you see at larger social gatherings or specific times of the year.

In the Western world, we are part of a culture that favors monotheism or henotheism. Monotheism is the worship of and belief in a single divine being. Henotheism is the worship of one specific divine being from a given pantheon. The idea of polytheism – the worship of many gods – can be difficult to wrap our heads around. Frequently, pagans will start with one deity but will quickly discover that they experience contact with other deities from that pantheon. I am Heathen and began working with the Norse goddess Freyja first. However, that quickly expanded to include more of the Norse pantheon. If we continue our social circle analogy, poly-theism is having many friendships within a given social circle as opposed to only one buddy on the bowling team. The experience of true polytheism is that you will work with many gods over the course of your life, some more frequently at certain times.

One thing that is also useful to cultivate is a "handshake relation-ship." If you spend a lot of time working and socializing with other pagans in your community, it's useful to become comfortable with the spirits and Gods they work with. For example, the co-authors of this book serve different deities who originate from different pantheons. However, both of us have had direct, respectful, and courteous contact with each other's gods. This is particularly useful when it comes to performing healings on others. Frequently in a spirit healing, the spirits, Gods, or ancestors of your client will appear. Learning to interact comfortably with spirits who are not your direct court is very useful.

STAYING CENTERED

When engaging in any form of spirit contact, it's important to remember to keep your wits about you. Just because a spirit contacts you does not mean you are obligated to it in any way. Every now and then, someone will say that because they've had an interaction with a deity, they now think they must become a dedicant – a worshiper or servant of that deity. That is simply not true.

One of the hardest concepts to wrap the modern, Western mind around is that spirits are *real*. They are not archetypes, not repressed personality traits (although more on that later), not some sort of trick or weird effect of the brain. Although they operate in a different plane of existence and have access to different information, they are very real sentient beings. Part of why it's difficult to comprehend the reality of the spirit world completely is that most westerners grew up in a culture of monotheistic Christianity. The god of that belief system is pretty distant and hands-off, and tends to speak through its priest class. The gods of many contemporary witches are the gods of the common people. They are more likely to contact everyday people directly as a result.

Another thing to bear in mind is that spirits have their own agendas. Some of those agendas are more benevolent than others. There are some spirits who really do just like to teach and help incarnated humans. Many of our spirit guides fall into this category. However, that is not universally true. The gods, in particular, tend to have goals they are working toward. They will sometimes try to convince humans to help them with this. Remember that although the gods are very able on the spiritual and energetic planes, they are less able to manipulate the physical realm. There are also some theories that part of what gives gods more influence is the energy of belief and worship. Cultivating human allies may increase their power if that theory is correct.

The reason we're talking about this is so that you know to stay centered and stand in your own power should a god contact you. Just because a deity appears in a meditation, journey, or ritual does not mean you are obligated to them in any way. Always be respectful and polite during spirit encounters, but do not feel that you need to obey commands or answer questions you are not comfortable with. This applies to any and all spirits – ancestors, guides, gods, everything. *You* are sovereign. You may ally yourself with whomever you choose, but that relationship is *your* choice. We are cocreators with our gods. If a god you are interacting with has a problem with that, you may politely show them the door. Relationships with the gods are similar to relationships with humans. If a god is abusive, LEAVE. They are not worthy of you, or of your devotion.

Know Thyself

In chapter two, 'Powers That Be' (page 24), you read about the importance of being aligned to your own True Voice.

> *"Before working with other spirits, be they embodied, disembodied (ancestral), or never embodied, the dialogue must begin with our most intimate spirit companion – our own spirit."*

> — ORION FOXWOOD, THE CANDLE AND THE
> CROSSROADS

Blackfeather emphasizes connection with the Self. The very first altar we create is to ourselves – it does not contain godforms or ancestral shrines. It's a shrine to you. There are many good reasons for that, but one of the main ones is that we need to reconnect with our own spirits – our souls, or higher selves.

Your spirit has a clear vision and deep knowledge for your life, uncontaminated by outside influence and upbringing. Getting into better communication with that knowing inner voice is absolutely vital. Knowing the sound and feel of how our spirit speaks will enable us to know when we hear a voice that is *not* ours. A consistent meditation or journey practice is the best way to cultivate contact with your spirit. Remember that movement meditation counts as meditation. Anything that quiets the chattering "monkey brain" and allows your deeper Self to speak will support your practice.

Mental health plays a huge role in safe spiritual alliance building. There is no one good, true way to know for certain that a voice you are experiencing isn't just part of your brain being a little fizzy. Using a divination system to confirm messages is a good practice. Some practitioners own a divinatory tool dedicated to the main spirits they work with specifically for this purpose. Any message that encourages self-harm should be disregarded. Likewise, particularly with gods, they are generally more interested in their goals than in the intricacies of your life. Having the gods point out that certain relationships, behaviors, or self-expectations are unhealthy can be really helpful. However, if a deity seems to be commanding you to change the way you dress or how you engage in human relationships (particularly sexual or romantic ones), it's worth seeking external confirmation and perhaps talking things out with a therapist. It's not that those things aren't possible, it's that they are less likely. Most gods don't care if you wear makeup or not. They do care about what you are doing to further their goals.

MAKING CONTACT

Relationships form one of two ways. Another being seeks you out and initiates contact, or you seek out a being and initiate contact.

Think of it like starting a conversation with a stranger. One of you has to say 'hi' first. During our spirit work exercises as well as earlier in this chapter, you have journeyed to your place of power to talk to different spirits. If you have been doing your journeywork at home, you have been cultivating a really great platform for connecting with spirits. Starting a co-creative relationship can be broken into steps. I am going to use creating a relationship with a deity as an example below, but this same set of steps works for land spirits, spirits of place, ancestors, and other spirits.

Research

What are you trying to do with your life? What areas of magick or spirituality interest you most? Learn about spirits who align with those areas or are skilled in the area of magick you are interested in. For example, if the healing arts interest you most, you might research Brighid, the Celtic goddess of healing, smithcraft and poetry. If you are interested in Divination, explore gods associated with prophecy like Frigg or Egeria. If you are currently undergoing or trying to initiate a big life transformation, gods associated with the underworld, death and rebirth might be a good fit. Remember to read several of the myths and overviews of the deities you are interested in. The gods of the ancient world are complex beings and can have problematic histories. You can also consider talking to or reading the work of people who are in co-creative relationships with those gods now. Your own experience may vary, of course, but the collective experience of people working with a given deity is generally pretty indicative of tone.

Offering

Once you have selected a deity you are interested in working with, learn what form of worship they prefer. What offerings do they like? How are they honored? Is there sacred poetry or music associated with them? Choose a simple way to get started. For example, if you are interested in cultivating a relationship with Athena, you could set up a small space on your altar to light a candle and make an offering of olive oil. If you choose to burn incense, you could use frankincense or myrrh. Then, you could say a prayer or litany of praise. Remember, you're starting a relationship. Think about the way you feel when someone you do not know comes up and asks for $5. You're more likely to stay in a conversation if a stranger begins interaction by telling you they like your hat, or sharing a piece of their story that they think aligns with yours. Try not to begin contact by making demands. Instead, simply offer the hand of friendship.

Listening/Observation

Create space for the spirit you are contacting to respond to your offering. This might be journeying or meditating after making your offering. It can also be watching for signs – animals, scents, and symbols associated with the spirit – that will frequently appear when the spirit in question responds. Continuing with the idea of connecting with Athena, if you get swooped past by an owl, have an article about the ruins of Athena's temple appear in your inbox, and find yourself craving olives, chances are good that Athena is reaching back.

Additionally, this is where divination tools come in. You can do a reading to see if your offering was accepted and if the spirit you are trying to communicate with is interested in forming a relationship with you. Using a divination system to confirm information we obtain spiritually is a wonderful habit to get into. If you work with one deity or pantheon regularly, you might consider having a divination tool dedicated specifically to them.

Lather, Rinse, Repeat

If the omens are good or you experience a positive response during your journeywork, then continue. Make offerings regularly. Find out what that spirit's holy days are and honor them. When you have worked with the spirit for some time, you can then begin to request guidance from them. Start simply by asking for advice – request their opinion on what your magickal focus should be, or how best to manage that annoying coworker.

Radio Silence

What if nothing happens? That occurs sometimes. The spirit you're trying to contact might be unavailable for some reason or may feel that they are not a good fit for you. That doesn't mean you should stop building your Spirit Court. It just means more research and exploration.

GETTING CONTACTED

Sometimes the spirits contact us first. Autumn, in particular, often features visitations from ancestors and those who have passed beyond the Veil. This can take the form of smelling someone's cologne or suddenly hearing their voice or cough or the specific jingle of their car keys. Many times, particularly in the darker part of the year, experiencing a mild visitation is just a loved one's way of saying "hi" while they're able to. However, if the pattern repeats, that ancestor or spirit might want to work with you.

Being contacted by other spirits can be similar – a string of coincidences is a common form of contact. Let's say Heimdallr is interested in cultivating a relationship with you. This could be present when you stumble upon an old ram figurine you forgot you had.

When you put it on a bookshelf, you realize you set it right next to a book of Norse mythology. Then, when you're scrolling social media, an article about Heimdallr pops up a few times. A few days later, a friend gifts you a horn. You begin to wonder if it's a message, so you consult your preferred divinatory system and get a positive reading.

Sometimes contact is more direct – this is the form that some of us joke about as being similar to getting mugged. A perfectly normal journey or meditation can suddenly take a dramatic turn and a deity will show up and start talking. Or, we have a vivid dream where that deity makes an appearance. In all cases, confirming with a divinatory tool is a good call. Some spirits will try to mask themselves as other beings in order to get attention. Making sure you're talking to Inanna and not some jumped up dead human in a goddess mask is a good idea.

After you've established that contact is being made, it's time to make a decision. Determine whether you would like to work with the spirit that contacted you. This is another place where research can be helpful. If you don't know much about the deity or spirit, definitely do your research. Learn about their history, abilities and preferences. If you would like to pursue a relationship, begin creating space for communication. This can follow the same format as Making Contact: create a little altar space for that spirit, make offerings, listen for feedback. If meditation or journeywork isn't your strong suit, use your preferred divinatory tool to "listen" to what they have to say.

Try to determine what the spirit wants from you. Remember that you do not have to agree to anything, or accept any "deals" they offer immediately. You can think about what you want from the relationship as well. One of the running jokes involving the gods of Heathenry is "never take the first deal offered."

If you decide you do not wish to work with the spirit that contacted you, politely decline the invitation. You can also request time to think about it, or ask for a "trial period" or "internship." It's a good idea to put time limits on any trial or internship.

SETTING BOUNDARIES

In all Spirit Court relationships, boundaries are important. Having a spirit or ancestor pop up next to your bed at 3 AM wanting to have a conversation with you is very frustrating. Create and communicate specific times and places for connection. A daily or weekly journey practice for that particular spirit can be a great way to address this. If a spirit shows up outside the chosen times and they are not trying to protect you from an emergency situation, simply redirect them to the agreed-upon meeting time.

GO SLOWLY

Much like falling in love, the rush of excitement that comes with spirit contact can be intoxicating. Remember that a healthy Spirit Court is built on solid foundations of friendship and cooperation. Allow your relationship to build and become stable before taking any vows or oaths. A minimum of a year's consistent practice and communication before even considering formal dedication is a safe guideline.

When you have finished your session, close the Ritual of Study as described on page 36.

CHAPTER SIXTEEN HOMEWORK

1. Practice the Blackfeather Self-Blessing, Grounding and Centering, and Shielding daily. Include seven minutes or more of meditation.

2. Continue your short divinatory practice, drawing one or two stones/cards/etc, and looking up the meanings of them. Remember, this is not a divination for the day. It is simply a way to help learn your divinatory tool's language.

3. Continue to explore Sacred Movement Practice. If you have a movement style that you enjoy, try to engage in it for a minimum of 10 minutes three times each week.

4. Journeywork: Continue your journeying practice using one of the journey audio tracks located at blackfeathermystery.com/recordings. You can use intentions for your journey from any previous chapter. Aim for three practice sessions per week.

5. Journaling Exercise: Select one to two of the simple, small steps you wrote out for your Life Sculpting work and make a plan for implementing them. Then do so.

6. Journaling Exercise: Consider how you feel about working with the gods. What form would you prefer your relationships with deities take?

7. Journaling Exercise: Think about unusual experiences you have had that might indicate spirit contact. What signs presented themselves? If you've had more than one experience, did those different situations have any similarities?

CHAPTER 17

GUISING

For this chapter, you will need this book, your Blackfeather oil, your Blackfeather altar, a device that can play both video and audio recordings online with a screen large enough to make out movement, your journal, a snack for afterwards, a space with plenty of room to move around, and your partner if you are working with one. All exercises can also be performed solitary. Your instructor is Irene and this chapter should take two to three hours to go through.

B egin this chapter by performing the opening of the Ritual of Study on page 20.

AN INTRODUCTION TO GUISING

One of the most powerful tools in a spirit worker's toolbox is shapeshifting – the transformation of the spiritual and energetic bodies into another form. When we Shapeshift, we become something other, something more authentic, or something more than what we are. Shapeshifting safely and effectively takes practice. One way to 'warm up' for shapeshifted consciousness is to use an intermediate form: Guising.

Guising shares some qualities with Shapeshifting, but it focuses on changing the energy body only. It is a conscious rather than consuming transition. As a result, it's a great technique for people who are not yet comfortable shapeshifting, have trouble shapeshifting, or have a hard time returning from a different shape. When we Guise, our core Self is still at the driver's wheel, unchanged. It's our energy body that shifts.

Guising is the state between acting and trance possession or shapeshifting. The practitioner remains in conscious control, and can choose which words to say or not say, but is also able to access information, aspects, qualities and identities outside their own.

Guising has a lot of uses in witchcraft. It allows us to:

- safely embody or inhabit a ritual character
- access reserves of confidence and strength we may not personally possess
- gain wisdom or insight through inhabiting a different point of view
- come into close contact with kinds of energy not as available to us in our usual energetic form
- move through certain planes/states of being disguised
- make ourselves more approachable by different Beings
- provide other Beings an opportunity to speak that they might not otherwise experience
- perform certain kinds of action/do certain kinds of Work not possible in your 'normal' body

We all Guise already to a certain extent – we have identities we step into for certain situations. The version of you that you embody at work is different than who you are at home. During your commute back to your home, you let that Guise – that work identity – slip off. This is not acting. When you're acting, you have a script and are using someone else's words. It's also not improv. During improv, you're consciously planning your next line. It's also not trance possession – your work self does not take over your mind and spirit.

Guising is a shifting of the energy body. We step into or shift into and then share another energetic form. For those of us who are left brain dominant, or who have concerns trusting other entities for trance possession, guising can be a wonderful tool. It can also be a step on the way to trance possession/shapeshifting depending on where you want your practice to take you.

Mirroring Exercise

Guising requires a certain amount of flexibility and movement freedom on the physical front. Frequently in guise, the new body may move or stand differently than you are used to. It's normal to come out of guise a little sore. One way to stretch these muscles and get your body accustomed to these feelings is to practice physically mirroring. It teaches us to breathe and move differently than we might otherwise. It also teaches us to work co-creatively with another Being – in this case, another human. This exercise can be performed two ways: solitary and with a partner.

Solitary Mirroring

On a device with a screen, please pull up the video located at blackfeathermystery.com/recordings. Place your device at a comfortable eye level so that you are not looking either sharply downward or sharply upward at the screen. Ensure that you have enough room to move your arms out to either side. When you play the video, begin by matching your breath cycle – lining up your inhale and exhale. Then, mirror the movement demonstrated in the video.

When the exercise has ended, record your experiences in your journal.

Partnered Mirroring

If you are working with a partner, move to an area in the room where the two of you can stand facing each other with enough room to move your arms out to either side. Begin by matching your breath cycle – lining up your inhale and exhale. Then, begin to mirror movement. Let this be a shared project. Rather than one person leading, allow the movement to grow organically. You may not even be able to tell who is directing a movement and who is following it. Set a timer for five minutes or use the journey track located at blackfeathermystery.com/recordings to play while you work.

When the exercise has ended, thank your partner and record your experiences in your journal. If you are working in a small group, rotate partners and practice the exercise again. At the close of the exercise, share your reflections with everyone you worked with.

SHAPING EXERCISE

Learning to inhabit another form through Guising includes using and manipulating energy in order to access and then move that new form. This exercise teaches energy shaping within the body. It also teaches us how to respond to cues about what a particular Guise needs in terms of movement and expression. As with mirroring, this exercise can be practiced both solitary and with a partner.

Solitary Shaping

Please bring up the guided audio track located at blackfeathermystery.com/recordings on a device with a good speaker. Find a place to practice where there's some space around you. You will want to be able to move your arms freely. If you are standing, you will also want to be able to step forward and back without hitting anything. The text of the audio track is located below in case you would like to record your own version of it.

Close your eyes and begin to draw up from the Earth, down from the Sky, or around you from the Web, as much energy as you can. Fill your body with that raw life energy. Breathe deeply as you gather the energy.

Keeping your eyes closed, extend your right arm up toward the sky at about a 45-degree angle. Keep your right hand relaxed with your palm facing the sky. Bring your left hand to your left hip. Turn your head toward the right and lift your chin as though you intend to gaze at your right hand. If you are standing, step your right foot out slightly and shift your weight onto your right foot.

Keeping your eyes closed, begin to move in the way your new shape moves. Maintain a light awareness of the space around you and go slowly so that you do not run into anything.

Come to stillness. Allow your body to return to its comfortable shape. Wiggle your fingers and toes, roll your shoulders, neck and head. Take a few deep breaths. Recenter yourself in your space for the next round if necessary.

Once again, draw up from the Earth, down from the Sky, or around you from the Web, as much energy as you can. Fill your body with that raw life energy. Breathe deeply as you gather the energy.

Keeping your eyes closed, reach both arms up and over your head, reaching slightly forward. Curl your hands toward the earth, allowing your fingers to curve into a gripping shape. Round your upper back and tilt your chin downward slightly. If you are performing this exercise standing, step your left foot forward slightly, bending the left knee.

Keeping your eyes closed, begin to move in the way your new shape moves. Maintain a light awareness of the space around you and go slowly so that you do not run into anything.

Come to stillness. Allow your body to return to its comfortable shape. Wiggle your fingers and toes, roll your shoulders, neck and head. Take a few deep breaths. Whenever you are ready, gently open your eyes.

Record your experiences in your journal.

Partnered Shaping

Partnered shaping involves light physical contact. Your partner will be physically positioning your arms, and may adjust your stance, or how you're holding your shoulders. You can stop the exercise at any point simply by opening your eyes or saying "stop." Find a place for this exercise that offers some space to move. You'll want to be able to freely move your arms and walk around. Choose who will be partner A and who will be partner B.

Please bring up the guided audio track located at blackfeathermystery.com/recordings on a device with a good speaker. The text of the audio track is located below in case you would like to record your own version of it.

Partner A, close your eyes and begin to draw up from the Earth, down from the Sky, or around you from the Web, as much energy as you can. Fill your body with that raw life energy.

Partner B, begin to draw that same life energy in, and then project it into your partner. This process builds up excess energy, which makes shaping much easier.

Partner A, keep your eyes closed and trust your partner to guide you with gentle touch or softly spoken words.

Partner B, begin to physically shape your partner into something they are not through gentle touch. You can move their limbs, turn their head and change their stance. You can use words if absolutely necessary.

Partner A, keeping your eyes closed, begin to move in the way your new shape moves. Partner B, spot your partner and keep them from bumping into anything using gentle touch or soft words.

Come to stillness. Partner A, Allow your body to return to its comfortable shape. Wiggle your fingers and toes, roll your shoulders, neck and head. Take a few deep breaths. Gently open your eyes.

We will do the same exercise, but reverse roles. Return the audio track to the beginning and rotate which person is Partner A and which is Partner B.

Thank your partner. Take a moment to check in with them and share reflections. Record your experiences in your journal.

GUISING EXERCISE

Find a space where you'll be free to move around a little bit. You'll want to be able to take a few steps and move your arms easily without hitting or running into anything. Once you've found that space, come to stillness.

For this Guise, we are going to connect with the energy of an Elemental – one of the smaller individuated emissaries of the Elemental egregores or gnars. Decide now which Element you would like to work with. This should be an Element you're comfortable with.

Please bring up the guided audio track located at blackfeathermystery.com/recordings on a device with a good speaker. The text of the audio track is below in case you would like to record your own version of it. Dim the lights in the room you are in so that you can still avoid any potential obstacles but are not subject to bright, glaring light.

Close your eyes and begin to breathe deeply. Starting at the top of your head, relax all the muscles in your head and face, then begin working your way down your body. Relax your neck and shoulders, your chest and back. Relax your belly. Relax your hips. Relax your legs all the way down to your feet and your arms all the way down to your fingertips.

A few feet in front of you, visualize the elemental emissary beginning to form in front of you. Take a nice deep breath in. On your exhale, breathe color and life into the elemental. As you continue to breathe, the elemental becomes more and more distinct on each exhale.

Reach your hands out, palm up, in front of you. Let the elemental step closer and place their hands in yours. When you choose to, step into the energy of that elemental.

Notice how your body shifts to take on this energetic form. Think about the elemental you are Guising. How does it move? What does it want? What feelings, images or emotions are surfacing?

Gently open your eyes to begin to see the world through the eyes of the elemental you are guising. Explore movement in guise – moving as the elemental you are Guising. Remember to go gently. Remember that you are in control this whole time – you can stop at any point and return to yourself. You are choosing to embody a particular energy.

Feel welcome to move around the room as your Guise dictates. A bell will sound when it is time to return.

Come to stillness. Close your eyes and begin to breathe deeply. Feel the guise you assumed beginning to slip off of you. Hold out your hands again, palms up. With every exhale, breathe out a little more of the elemental. See it forming in front of you once more, touching your hands.

With a final exhale, breathe out the last of the guise. Gently release contact with the elemental. Thank them for their cooperation with you. Watch them fade back into their Elemental realm.

Take a deep breath. Wiggle your fingers and toes. Rub your arms, your face, your belly. Perform your Return to Self gesture. When you are ready, gently open your eyes. Record your experiences in your journal.

GROUNDING AND CENTERING

After Guising or any other intense energy work, thoroughly grounding and centering is important self-care.

A recording of this Grounding and Centering is available at blackfeathermystery.com/recordings.

Close your eyes and allow your breath to deepen and lengthen. Consciously relax your body, starting at the top of your head and working your way down to your neck and shoulders...your chest and back...your lower back and hips...your legs all the way to your toes...your arms all the way to your fingertips.

Draw your awareness to your heart center. Notice a green glow radiating from your heart. This is your life force – raw prana or chi: the magick that animates you and all living things. Become aware of the bright glow of life within you. You might see or sense that energy pulsing in time with your heartbeat.

Your heart center is part of a web of life extending in all directions. Become aware of the lines of energy connecting you to other life. They stretch in all directions – above, below, out to either side... These pathways hum with creation energy – the raw force of life. Allow some of the energy from the web to flow toward you. Let that green life-energy replenish your heart center, then expand to heal and recharge any areas of your body that need it.

When you feel full and connected, turn your palms to face up or out and gather the extra energy still flowing toward you by slowly sweeping your arms from your sides to up over your head, allowing the palms to touch. Draw your hands down to your heart, resting them on your chest. Feel your body incorporating that energy and returning to itself.

Whenever you are ready, take a deep breath and exhale on a sigh. Gently open your eyes.

If you are still feeling a little spacey or disconnected, eat something to help you reintegrate with your body. Salty or spicy flavors are good for becoming fully seated in normal consciousness again.

When you have finished your session, close the Ritual of Study as described on page 36.

CHAPTER SEVENTEEN HOMEWORK

1. Practice the Blackfeather Self-Blessing, Grounding and Centering, and Shielding daily. Include seven minutes or more of meditation.

2. Continue your short divinatory practice, drawing one or two stones/cards/etc, and looking up the meanings of them. Remember, this is not a divination for the day. It is simply a way to help learn your divinatory tool's language.

3. Continue to explore Sacred Movement Practice. If you have a movement style that you enjoy, try to engage in it for a minimum of 10 minutes three times each week.

4. Journeywork: Continue your journeying practice using one of the journey audio tracks located at blackfeathermystery. com/recordings. You can use intentions for your journey from any previous chapter. Aim for three practice sessions per week.

5. Journaling Exercise: Evaluate your overall experience with guising. What other elements would you like to guise as? Consider other Beings you might be interested in experiencing or connecting with through guise.

6. Journaling Exercise: Reflect on how your first step(s) of Elemental Life Sculpting are going. Where are you encountering satisfaction and pleasure? Where are you encountering resistance?

CHAPTER 18

BEGINNING SHAPESHIFTING

For this chapter, you will need this book, your Blackfeather oil, your Blackfeather altar, a device that can play a recording online (if so desired), a snack for afterward, plenty of space to move around in, and your journal. This chapter includes some journeywork, so a comfortable place to sit where you will be relaxed but not in danger of falling asleep can be useful. This chapter also includes shapeshifting, so uninterrupted study time is important. Your instructor is Caine and this chapter should take two to three hours to go through.

B egin this chapter by performing the opening of the Ritual of Study on page 20.

THE THINGS WE BECOME

In discussing shapeshifting, it is important that we fully integrate the very simple fact that we (our core selves) are not, in fact, humans. Rather, we are powerful immortal souls currently inhabiting a human body. Being able to internalize this understanding will allow a better grasp of all the aspects of the practice called shapeshifting.

As a person, you are an energetically fluid being. This means that the energy you present will shift and change based on a number of factors. Sometimes it will be unconscious, like the vibe we put out when we're in a bad mood. Most people can recall times when they have **felt** as much as seen someone sitting in a waiting room, or standing in line, and just known that the individual in question was one refund denial away from becoming the Incredible Hulk. Other times, our energy shift is very conscious. When people get home from work, they no longer talk to people in their "business voice" (much to everyone's relief, I'm sure).

The art of shapeshifting is taking that concept of fluidity and leveraging it in some fantastically powerful ways. This practice allows us to set aside the "human" aspect of our existence and experience our world through a completely new lens. Shapeshifting can be used for protection, healing, and even pleasure.

Shapeshifting not only has different uses, but it also has different levels of immersion and complexity. Each level has its purpose, and can be used to great effect. However, the further down the rabbit hole you go, the more risks are involved. It needs to be understood that this is very much a "walk before you run" kind of skill set. Shapeshifting should be practiced frequently by those wanting to experience what it has to offer.

But why even bother?

Why practice shapeshifting at all? First and foremost, it is powerful protective magic. Merging, even just with your own

Within (more on that below), will help to provide a barrier between yourself and the rest of whatever plane of existence you are journeying to. This is especially important for traveling within the middle realm where you are more likely to run into shells (the leftover bits of ego after a person dies). Second, shapeshifting deepens our relationship with our spirit helpers. It allows your energies to harmonize with theirs over time, which is necessary to advance your practices together. To put a new spin on an old quote, "two heads are better than one." Everything from basic energy work to full-blown rituals can be enhanced by the extra boost of power shapeshifting can give us.

WITHIN VS. WITHOUT

Within shapeshifting, the first thing to understand is the source of whatever shape you are attempting. There are only two places we can get those shapes from: inside or outside of us.

The exercises in this chapter use that which is already within the matrix of our own soul. It is energy we already possess, so it is already familiar and safe to tap into. This allows us to explore our own potential before delving into the deeper end of the pool.

Many people have heard of "spirit animals." Differing schools of thought exist about them, and you will undoubtedly hear a lot of mixed information. The specific phrase "spirit animal" is also associated with cultural appropriation of First Nations traditions. A more accurate description for the allies we work with is "spirit helper" or "spirit guide" since our spirit allies take many forms – not just those of animals. There is a simple hierarchy we will be using as our shared vocabulary for this work.

Spirit Helper. A Helper is a spirit that may or may not be temporary, or will serve in a single or limited capacity. A spirit worker may retrieve a helper for their client that can stick around for a period to assist the client's continued healing.

Power Spirit. A Power Spirit is a relationship with a spirit that is long-lasting, potentially transcending multiple lifetimes. They directly influence/inform your practice by either teaching you specific skills or encouraging you down particular paths of study. Power Spirits also are usually quick to lend their own energy to your magic, becoming a sort of second battery. Beware NOT to abuse this relationship, however, as having a fatigued or disempowered Power Spirit can leave the practitioner vulnerable.

The Within. Our Within (capital W) is a non-human form that our own spirit has either most often or most recently reincarnated as. When I ask the spirits about this one, the answers as to the specific origin of the Within vary. This is a powerful piece of who we are, and will be the foundation for your shapeshifting practice. It often initially presents itself as a being separate from us until we are more fully integrated with it.

TUNING, BLENDING, INTEGRATING

Our bodies are here to serve us as anchors to the physical realm. The patterns of behavior we develop while in our bodies are partly from genetics, partly from our environment, and partly from the legacy of lifetimes our souls have experienced. The way we experience the world is that of a human being. While we cannot change the flesh (at least not to the extent entertainment media portrays shapeshifting), or the path that led us to this moment, we can alter the way our spirit interacts with the world around us. This is the true essence of shapeshifting. Not just walking on all fours, or howling at the moon (though both are a good time), but BEING the shape we choose in the most profound way possible.

There are three main ways to shift our spirit.

Tuning. Tuning is the first and easiest method. It involves working with what we already have/are. Conceptually, you are shifting the frequency of your spirit. If you can imagine all the possibilities of shapes we can take as a list of radio stations, you are tuning in to the frequency of your chosen shape in order to experience it.

Blending. This is the first of two methods that tap into energies from outside ourselves. Instead of the frequency metaphor, a more appropriate explanation of blending would be putting a single drop of food coloring into a glass of water. That sort of billowing effect, where the color begins to stretch and flow within the water, is the addition of a spirit helper to your own energy. At this point, the two beings are still separate, even if the lines are a bit blurry.

Integrating. Integration is the most complex form of shapeshifting. At this point, you've stirred the glass. No longer is it water, or dye, but a glass of colored water. Two separate beings have merged to become a third. No longer am I myself, no longer is the spirit itself. We are a new and different being. This sort of experience takes a deep level of mutual trust and understanding between you and the spirit with which you are integrating. To attempt this without both a mastery of the other forms of shapeshifting and an established relationship with the spirit is incredibly dangerous for both of you.

It is important to note that Shapeshifting is far easier and safer to experiment with while journeying. The practice of "blending" is also often referred to as "merging" during a journey. Merging is much simpler, as it is entirely energetic and does not involve a physical experience here in the material realm.

DOING THE WORK

Now that you have all of this new information swirling in your head, let's get drumming! For the first two exercises below, please either use the 10 minute journey track located at blackfeathermystery.com/recordings or set a timer for ten minutes each time and use your own rattle or drum to induce trance. Please have a journal and something to write with nearby. Remember that you can repeat journeys more than once and that it is perfectly fine to pop into and out of trance briefly in order to remember the questions you want to ask or write down answers you receive.

Journey #1: As mentioned earlier, the easiest route to shapeshifting is by working with what we already have. For this first journey, set your intention to go to your place of power. Once there, conjure a reflective surface of whatever sort feels right to you. Then, stand in front of your reflection and ask to be shown your Within. Once you can see it, ask the following questions:

What are you exactly? (In case the image is unclear or unfamiliar)

What energies or powers do you possess?

How can I better tap into you during my daily life?

Write down your answers either during your journey or when you return. Remember, this information will start to fade quickly upon returning to normal consciousness. Do not wait to record the information you were given.

Journey #2: Set an intention to return once more to your place of power. This time, instead of a mirror, call to your Within to appear fully before you. Once it does, embrace it, and allow yourself to take on the shape of your Within. Together, the two of you may run, fly, swim and play until you hear the callback in the drumming track (or the timer going off if you are using a drum or rattle). At that time, return to your normal shape, and then return to your physical body.

Record your experiences in your journal when you return.

Journey #3: For this journey, use the 20 minute journey track located at blackfeathermystery.com/recordings. Make sure you are in a space where you can move around a little bit and where you will not be disturbed for the length of this exercise. Lower the light levels a bit before you begin.

Set an intention to go back to your place of power and invite your Within to appear. Then, gather your Within up in your arms and draw it into yourself. As you do so, you will once again take on the form of your Within. Then, *return to your body* as this new shape you have taken.

For the remainder of the journey, take some time to settle into this different existence. Notice what, if anything, is different about it. You may smell, see, or feel things differently. You may notice a sense of extra appendages (wings, a tail, etc). Feel free to stand, or move around a bit, to further your experience.

When you hear the callback drum pattern, come to stillness and sit down. Gently release your Within and return to your normal shape.

Record your experiences in your journal.

Grounding and Centering

After shapeshifting as well as guising, a thorough grounding and centering is necessary to help us reintegrate with consensus physical reality. A recording of this Grounding and Centering is available at blackfeathermystery.com/recordings, the text is available on page 245 in Chapter Seventeen.

If you are still feeling a little spacey or disconnected, eat something to help you reintegrate with your body. Salty or spicy flavors are good for becoming fully seated in normal consciousness again.

When you have finished your session, close the Ritual of Study as described on page 36.

CHAPTER EIGHTEEN HOMEWORK

1. Practice the Blackfeather Self-Blessing, Grounding and Centering, and Shielding daily. Include seven minutes or more of meditation or journeying.

2. Continue your short divinatory practice, drawing one or two stones/cards/etc and looking up the meanings of them. Remember, this is not a divination for the day. It is simply a way to help learn your divinatory tool's language.

3. Continue to explore Sacred Movement Practice. If you have a movement style that you enjoy, try to engage in it for a minimum of 10 minutes three times each week.

4. Journaling Exercise: Evaluate your overall experience with shapeshifting. Which journey was the most accessible for you? Which journey was the most challenging? What shape does your Within take, and what does it tell you about yourself?

5. Exercise and Reflection: Tune into or Blend with your Within during a regular journey practice. What changed? How did your experience differ from journeys when you were not Tuned or Blended?

CHAPTER 19

CLOSING RITUAL

Practice may not make perfect, but it tends to make permanent. Over the course of studying this book, you developed a daily altar practice that includes grounding, centering, and shielding. You spent time blessing and empowering yourself. You began to shape your life to fit your true nature. You developed a Sacred Movement practice and a journeywork practice. You learned a pattern for creating sacred space that can be used anywhere, with almost any working. You began your relationship with the spirits and cultivated spirit allies. You learned to direct energy and to protect yourself magically. You began building your spirit working toolkit. You performed ceremonies and learned techniques for effective spellcasting and ritual creation. You started on the path to shapeshifting.

In short, you earned your wings. Take a moment to look back to where you were when you began this book. Committing to a path of study takes focus, drive, and enthusiasm. Enjoy the growth you have experienced and feel pride in your accomplishments and your dedication.

Supplies for the Closing Ritual

Please gather/prepare

- Your Blackfeather altar. You will specifically need the mirror and candle for this working.
- Your bottle of Blackfeather oil.
- A piece of paper with the following Words of Power in large print/font – you will be working in low light:

I am beautiful because (3 – 6 reasons)
I am powerful because (3 – 6 reasons)
I am strong because (3 – 6 reasons)
I am compassionate because (3 – 6 reasons)
I am _____ (name)

- Any ritual attire you would like to wear for this ritual
- Your journal and something to write with
- A device that can play a recording found online (if so desired)
- A snack for afterwards (this ritual includes guising)

Remember that words spoken in ritual space have power. Please give your preparation plenty of consideration.

Also, before the unseen demons you fight decide to pipe up, you ARE beautiful. You ARE powerful. You ARE strong. And you ARE compassionate. You would not have reached this part of the course otherwise. Blackfeather self-selects for a certain kind of witch. If you're reading these words, guess what? You're it.

For the section with your name, you may use any name you like. It can be the name you go by, your magickal or Working name, or it can be a name you wish to be known by going forward.

Once you have gathered your supplies, perform the opening of the Ritual of Study on page 20.

Stand or sit before your altar and take the following journey. An audio recording of it can be found at:

blackfeathermystery.com/recordings.

Journey to the Mirror

Close your eyes and allow your breath to deepen and lengthen. Consciously relax your body, starting at the top of your head and working your way down to your neck and shoulders.your chest and back...your lower back and hips...your legs all the way to your toes...your arms all the way to your fingertips.

Draw your awareness to your heart center. Notice a green glow radiating from your heart. This is your life force – raw prana or chi: the magick that animates you and all living things. Become aware of the bright glow of life within you. You might see or sense that energy pulsing in time with your heartbeat.

Your heart center is part of a web of life extending in all directions. Become aware of the lines of energy connecting you to other life. They stretch in all directions – above, below, out to either side... These pathways hum with creation energy – the raw force of life. Allow some of the energy from the web to flow toward you. Let that green life-energy replenish your heart center, then expand to heal and recharge any areas of your body that need it.

Notice a nexus of that green, fiery energy forming in front of you. It begins to take the shape of a ring of green flame around a center well of darkness. As you watch, the ring begins to expand, moving into a more oblong shape. The dark center takes on a metallic sheen and you realize that a mirror is taking shape before you. Right now, it shows nothing.

When the mirror has finished forming, set an intention to see your empowered witch self. Tell the mirror that is what you wish to see, and touch the surface of the glass. The glass will ripple, and then show you what you have requested.

Look at your reflection. Notice how your witch self stands, how they carry themselves. Notice the differences and the similarities to your-self right now.

Allow the mirror's frame to expand until it becomes a doorway. Take a nice deep breath in. On your exhale, breathe color and life into your witch self. Welcome your witch self to step through the doorway, to stand in front of you. As you continue to breathe, your witch self becomes more and more distinct on each exhale.

Reach your hands out, palm up, in front of you. Let your witch self step closer and place their hands in yours. When you choose to, step into or draw toward you, your witch self.

Notice how your body shifts to take on this energetic form. Gently open your eyes and see the world through this guise.

The Closing Ritual

Light the candle, uncover your mirror, and position it so that you can look into your own eyes. Uncap your Blackfeather oil or bottle of scent you are using. Look into your own eyes in the reflection. As you look into your eyes in the mirror, allow a feeling of love and acceptance to rise in you. Look into your own eyes with compassion and pride.

Read the Words of Power off of your piece of paper – the Words that start with "I am beautiful because…" and as often as you can, look into your own eyes as you do so.

Then, put some of your anointing oil onto your finger. Say aloud the self-blessing below. It is similar to the one you have been using all along, but not the same.

I bless my body with strength. I am manifesting my own power. (anoint your shoulders)

I bless my mind with focus. I am realizing my own wisdom. (anoint your third eye)

I bless my spirit with vitality. I am accessing my own potency. (anoint your heart)

I bless my blood with memory. I am claiming my own heritage. (anoint your wrists)

I bless my path with mystery. I am revealing that which is greater than myself. (anoint your legs or feet)

I bless my Self with sovereignty. I am affirming my own ascendency. (draw a crown around your head)

By the Powers who watch over me, by the Powers living within me, so it is, so it shall be.

I am _____ (name)

Notice how you feel. Take a little time to record your experience with the closing ritual in your journal.

Although we can embody our ideal selves for windows of time, it is neither reasonable nor possible to be that self *all* the time, as much as we would like to. You now know how to access and embody your Empowered Witch self. Simply repeat the guising process with that Self when you wish to access that particular aspect.

Gently release your Empowered Witch self. Close your eyes and begin to breathe deeply. Feel the guise beginning to slip off of you. Hold out your hands again, palms up. With every exhale, breathe out a little more of your Empowered Witch self. See that Self forming in front of you once more, touching your hands.

With a final exhale, breathe out the last of the guise. Gently release contact and allow the vision of your Empowered Witch self to fade.

Take a deep breath. Wiggle your fingers and toes. Rub your arms, your face, your belly. Perform your Return to Self gesture. When you are ready, gently open your eyes.

Close the Ritual of Study as described on page 36.

The Magpie in Flight

You now have access to a diverse magickal toolkit, spirit helpers and guides, and your Empowered Witch self. Your foundation for the practice of witchcraft and spirit work is solid, and is the one I wish I'd had a little over two decades ago when I got started.

The Winding Path of paganism is a long, varied, and interesting one. There are so many things to learn and experience. Your path will be unique, just like you. As a result, there are only a handful of axioms that apply across the board. However, one that is true is "That which is fed increases." Continue your daily spiritual practice. Continue your weekly journeying, sacred movement practice, and divination practice. These habits and patterns will keep you strong, flexible, connected, and growing.

Begin to think about what you would like to learn next. Your studies here have prepared you well for a focus on any number of areas within witchcraft and spirit work. What parts of this book did you love the most? You could choose to expand your healing abilities, your allies in the spiritual realm, your divination skills, spellcraft, or ritual arts, and so much more. Remember, fire needs fuel to burn, and learning is a lifelong engagement.

May the Gods bless you,
may the Ancestors watch over you,
may the Spirits guide you,
and may you feel your own power growing ever stronger within you.
So it is, so it shall be.

Appendix

Works Cited

Foxwood, O. (2012). Chapter Two - The Three Paths to Cultivating the Spirit. In *The candle and The CROSSROADS: A book of Appalachian CONJURE and Southern root-work* (pp. 21), Weiser Books.

Andrews, T. (2004) Chapter One. In *Nature-Speak: Signs, Omens and Messages in Nature* (pp. 27), Dragonhawk Publishing.

Training and Practices

Labyrinth Work: The Visioning, Releasing, and Receiving technique of labyrinth work was learned from Tracy Andryc of One Path Labyrinth Ventures. Other Labyrinth information and approaches in this text evolved from Labyrinth facilitator training with the Labyrinth Guild of New England.

Guising Techniques: The techniques supporting Guising as well as the Return to Self Gesture were learned from Moira Ashleigh and Duncan Eagleson through Corvid Clan Work.

INDEX

A

Altar, 4, 5, 7, 13, 14, 18, 20, 21, 22, 25, 36, 38, 51, 60, 73, 85, 88, 102, 115, 125, 127, 138, 142, 153, 165, 175, 183, 186, 191, 198, 203, 215, 225, 227, 230, 233, 244, 253, 254

Ancestors, 9, xv, 23, 31, 81, 102, 105, 126, 157, 202, 211, 218, 223, 225, 227, 229

B

Blackfeather Oil, 15, 18, 20, 38, 60, 73, 88, 102, 115, 125, 139, 142, 153, 165, 175, 182, 186, 198, 215, 233, 244, 254, 256

Blackfeather Temple, 18, 22, 23, 36

C

Circle Casting Chant, 21

D

Daily Practice, xviii, 5, 6, 7, 12, 13, 20, 21, 25, 27, 87, 112

Deities, xv, 23, 34, 89, 128, 157, 223, 227, 232

> Gods, 9, xv, xvii, 4, 29, 30, 32, 34, 35, 45, 46, 61, 88, 128, 194, 199, 212, 215, 216, 223, 259

Devotional Witchcraft, 215

Divination, 5, 85, 137, 140, 227

> Tool Consecration, 85

E

Elemental Life Sculpting, 6, 142, 144, 152, 164, 174, 184, 185, 197, 243

Elements and Elementals, 4, 61, 216

> Elemental Meditation, 63

Empowerment, 75, 107, 126, 127, 128, 131, 133, 134, 140, 141, 155, 156, 161, 184

Energy work, 38, 48, 49, 59, 76, 128, 170, 172, 174, 241, 246

> Directing Energy, 20, 50
> Energetic Anatomy, 39, 41, 43
> Energy Body Balancing, 43, 59
> Raising Energy, 47, 50, 81
> The Three Bodies, 28, 132

G

Ghosts, 30

Grounding and Centering, 8, 6, 9, 10, 17, 20, 37, 47, 59, 72, 87, 100, 114, 123, 140, 152, 163, 173, 176, 179, 185, 196, 214, 231, 241, 243, 250, 252

Guided Meditations, 19, 34, 113, 209

Guising, 8, 233, 234, 235, 236, 239, 241, 261

    Guising Exercise, 8, 239

H

Healing, xvi, xvii, xx, 9, 15, 16, 24, 49, 55, 56, 58, 76, 80, 81, 82, 83, 87, 102, 103, 104, 105, 106, 128, 156, 158, 170, 173, 174, 177, 178, 211, 227, 245, 246, 258

J

Journeywork, xviii, xix, 1, 12, 119, 134, 153, 155, 165, 169, 215, 226, 228, 230, 244, 253

    Place of Power, 19, 20, 23, 36, 169, 190, 222
    State of Consciousness, 154, 155, 158, 160

L

Labyrinth, 34, 175, 176, 177, 178, 179, 180, 181, 182, 183, 184, 185, 261

Drawing a Labyrinth, 179
Labyrinth as a Ritual Tool, 7, 180

M

Meditation, 12, 13, 15, 19, 23, 34, 60, 62, 63, 65, 102, 109, 112, 113, 114, 125, 140, 146, 149, 152, 163, 168, 173, 177, 178, 185, 196, 214, 224, 225, 226, 230, 231, 243, 252

Mirror Journey, 6, 134

Mirroring Exercise, 8, 235

P

Protection, xiii, 82

Apotropaics, 5, 74, 75
Shielding, xviii, 12, 90, 91, 93, 95, 100, 253

R

Return to Self Mudra, 48, 49, 59

Ritual of Study, 4, 18, 19, 22, 36, 37, 38, 59, 60, 71, 73, 87, 88, 100, 102, 114, 115, 123, 125, 140, 142, 152, 153, 163, 165, 173, 175, 184, 186, 196, 198, 213, 215, 231, 233, 243, 244, 251, 254, 258

Closing, 4, 19, 36, 37, 59, 253, 256
Opening, 20

Rituals, 4, 14, 24, 32, 40, 48, 62, 82, 92, 151, 199, 200, 202, 203, 204, 211, 212, 214, 246

Spirits, 9, xv, xvii, 24, 25, 26, 28, 29, 30, 32, 35, 37, 60, 61, 77, 78, 79, 81, 83, 88, 89, 94, 98, 100, 104, 105, 107, 121, 156, 157, 158, 195, 204, 215, 216, 217, 218, 219, 223, 224, 225, 226, 227, 229, 230, 247, 253

Corporeal Spirits, 28, 29, 45
Harmful spirits, 75
Incorporeal Spirits, 29, 32
Nature Spirits, 32, 33
Noncorporeal Spirits, 32
Spirits of Place, 32, 33
The Good Folk, 28, 33, 35

Statement of Purpose, 4, 19, 24

W

Wards, 77, 80, 98, 100

CPSIA information can be obtained
at www.ICGtesting.com
Printed in the USA
BVHW081058190522
637501BV00002B/12

9 781737 729266